Public Speaking

Speak Like a Pro

How to Destroy Social Anxiety, Develop Self-Confidence, Improve Your Persuasion Skills and Become a Master Presenter

Public Speaking

PUBLISHED BY: James W. Williams

© Copyright 2019 - All rights reserved.

The content contained within this book may not be reproduced, duplicated or transmitted without direct written permission from the author or the publisher.

Under no circumstances will any blame or legal responsibility be held against the publisher, or author, for any damages, reparation, or monetary loss due to the information contained within this book. Either directly or indirectly.

Legal Notice:

This book is copyright protected. This book is only for personal use. You cannot amend, distribute, sell, use, quote or paraphrase any part, or the content within this book, without the consent of the author or publisher.

Disclaimer Notice:

Please note the information contained within this document is for educational and entertainment purposes only. All effort has been executed to present accurate, up to date, and reliable, complete information. No warranties of any kind are declared or implied. Readers acknowledge that the author is not engaging in the rendering of legal, financial, medical or professional advice. The content within this book has been derived from various sources. Please consult a licensed professional before attempting any techniques outlined in this book.

By reading this document, the reader agrees that under no circumstances is the author responsible for any losses, direct or indirect, which are incurred as a result of the use of information contained within this document, including, but not limited to, — errors, omissions, or inaccuracies

Table of Contents

Your Free Gift 5
Book Review 6
Introduction 9

PART ONE: THE BATTLE WITHIN 15
CHAPTER ONE: The Introvert's Bubble 16
CHAPTER TWO: CROWDED SPACES 30
CHAPTER THREE: BUILDING BLOCKS OF CONFIDENCE 45
CHAPTER FOUR: ELIMINATING OBSTACLES 58

PART TWO: SETTING THE STAGE 72
CHAPTER FIVE: UNDERSTANDING THE WHYS 73
CHAPTER SIX: CHOOSING YOUR FIGHTS CAREFULLY 87
CHAPTER SEVEN: LOOKING THE PART ... 104

PART THREE: GOING FOR GOLD 119
CHAPTER EIGHT: THE ART OF PUBLIC SPEAKING 120

CHAPTER NINE: MANAGING YOUR STAGE 134
CHAPTER TEN: THE TOOLS OF THE TRADE 144

CLOSING..152
Thank you..155

Your Free Gift

As a way of saying thanks for your purchase, I wanted to offer you a free bonus E-book called ***Bulletproof Confidence,*** exclusive to the readers of this book.

To get instant access, just go to:

https://theartofmastery.com/confidence/

Inside the book, you will discover:

- What are shyness & social anxiety, and the psychology behind them
- Simple yet powerful strategies for overcoming social anxiety
- Breakdown of the traits of what makes a confident person
- Traits you must DESTROY if you want to become confident
- Easy techniques you can implement TODAY to keep the conversation flowing
- Confidence checklist to ensure you're on the right path of self-development

Book Review

Have you been called upon to speak at an event recently and the thought of doing it is giving you sleepless nights? Are you looking to make your mark in the world of public speaking but have no clue where to begin? Whether you are speaking as the best man at your friend's wedding, leading a presentation by your team at the next board meeting or speaking to an audience of eager people, this book, *Public Speaking: Speak Like a Pro; How to Destroy Social Anxiety, Develop Self-Confidence, Improve Your Persuasion Skills and Become a Master Presenter* is just what you need.

Delve into the core issues that could be affecting your self-esteem. Get practical tips on how to deliver your speech and overcome your social anxiety with the wealth of information made available in one accessible platform. Unlock the amazing potential within you in quick and easy steps. In this book you will find:

- Tips on getting you out of your comfort zone
- Effective ways to define yourself as a public speaker

- A guide to creating a winning strategy for your presentation no matter the occasion
- How to dress like a professional public speaker
- Tools that will help you succeed in your presentation
- And much more!

The average public speaker earns as much as $104,000 annually in the US. The guys in the upper echelon of that statistic have annual earnings that go as high as $300,000 within the same timeframe. In essence, this is a profession that is valued by a lot of people and if done right, it can get create a sustainable income that can set you up for the rest of your life. But the road that takes you from where you are to the point where you are raking in a six-figure income annually is paved with obstacles that not many books or public speaking resources have addressed.

This book, Public Speaking: Speak Like a Pro; How to Destroy Social Anxiety, Develop Self-Confidence, Improve Your Persuasion Skills and Become a Master Presenter, provides you with a wholesome perspective on becoming a public speaker that is effective, practical and insightful. The objective of this book is not just to make you a public speaker, but one who is bold enough to stand on any stage and share their truth with their audience. Your fears should not have the power to impede your dreams. Reach into yourself and unleash your full potential with this book one page at a time. Don't let that incredible talent that you have go to waste. Turn over to the next page and begin the next chapter of your life!

James W. Williams

Introduction

I remember the first time I got on stage to speak. I was only six-years-old and I was meant to be a very mean tree in a school play. The key to skillfully playing that part lied in me wearing a scowl for most of that scene and delivering my line (just one line) perfectly. I attended all the rehearsals. I practiced my line. I was going to crush it on that day. After wearing my costume, my teacher called me the cutest mean tree ever. I was convinced that I had this locked down. But when the time came to deliver, I completely froze. Even now, I can see the whole thing playing out before me in slow motion. First, the tree costume suddenly became too hot for me so I became sweaty and fidgety. I heard some people in the audience laugh (perhaps thinking it was all part of the play) and this agitated me even more. Poor Billy (who played the prince) didn't notice how unstable I was as he walked right into one of my extended roots and then tripped.

Billy survived the fall. I didn't survive the humiliation. Stories about my "epileptic" stage antics were pedaled throughout the whole school and it felt like everywhere I went, people mocked and made fun of me. Thankfully, my parents moved us to another city which meant a new school, new friends and a clean start. But the new environment did nothing to assuage my growing paranoia around people. Every time I was asked to speak to someone, even those I was familiar with, I would clam up and start sweating profusely. My father thought it was an age thing so he assured me that as I got older, those feelings would pass. They didn't. Things only intensified to the point that I was living as a total recluse. This was the lowest point of my life. It has been over two decades since that incident and my life has undergone a complete 360. I am now an author, speaker and a successful businessman.

So how did I go from James the hermit to this person who loves and lives for the spotlight? People shouldn't be able to change that drastically, right? Well, wrong. I am living proof of that and I am excited to share my journey and my process. It started with my first job as an independent telemarketer for an insurance company. The job suited me because my interaction with people was limited to phone conversations. All I had to do was cold-call people and make a pitch. I know that people hated getting those calls but I actually enjoyed it because I was the one making that call. This led to a pretty interesting discovery about myself...I am an incredible salesman. Underneath that painfully shy exterior was a guy with an amiable personality and a voice that made people feel at ease. It was like discovering that I had this superpower.

Subsequently, I was called in by my superiors to take on more responsibilities, one of which was to speak to a team of telemarketers and share my success tips with them. Oh boy! I was immediately transported back to my nightmare moment on stage. There was no way I was going to willingly put myself through that horror show. However, my supervisors were not having it. I had one month to prepare for that speaking event. In my head, that meant I had one month to get my affairs in order and move to another city. If my budget could afford it, I wouldn't have minded moving to another country altogether. When I got back home that day, I shared the news with my dad. I also told him what I planned to do. He simply nodded just like all the wise dads I knew and then asked me a single question: "How long are you going to keep running, James?"

This question prompted a flashback to my high school and college years. Every time I was assigned speaking tasks, I ran away from them. I didn't see it as running away at the time. But as I stood there with my dad, those memories came to me in flashes. It was like a montage in a very bad movie. I knew I had to stop running and that moment seemed like the perfect opportunity to begin. I was terrified. But I started by doing some research on public speaking. I found a few courses that promised to transform me into a prolific speaker in a month if I had at least $500. At my age and money bracket back then, it was like asking me to pay millions. Obviously, that route wasn't going to do it for me. I had to comb through hours of videos and articles on the subject for information on public speaking. A lot of it was vague or written to sell a product or service. None of it delved into the subject completely.

I went through this process for weeks and by the time the day for my speaking event came, I was maybe 35% ready. I would like to say that I went through that event like a boss and totally nailed it but no, that was not the case. Nobody fell on the stage that day and even though I was drenched in sweat by the time I was done, I made it through with a semblance of my dignity intact. However, in the notes I made after the event, I compared my performance there to mowing a lawn. I just kept droning on like a lawn mower and chopping through my points in the same manner. It was bland, boring and uninspiring. There were a lot of cringe-worthy moments but I had one big takeaway from it: It heralded the beginning of my public speaking career.

More than eleven years later, I have worked on a lot of projects that involved me speaking on stage in front of peers and colleagues. I still get hit by stage fright every time I get close to the stage but getting over my fears and climbing on stage anyway has gotten easier with each try. If you are reading this, there is a part of you that identifies with my journey. You have a gift that needs to be shared with the world but your shyness, anxiety and lack of self-confidence have enabled your decision to keep to yourself. I am going to ask you the same question my dad asked me: How long are you going to keep running?

You have the chance to step out of your shell and there is no better time to begin than now. Before you flip to the next chapter, here are tips on how to use this book successfully:

1. Take your time to read through each chapter and process the information. Diligence— not speed—is required here.
2. Make side notes as you study. This helps you assimilate better.
3. Complete the exercises at the end of each chapter. They nudge you gently out of your comfort zone.
4. Put the information that you get to practice. Practice is the key to perfecting your craft.
5. Maintain a positive outlook. This feeds your esteem and fuels your determination to see this through to the end.

I want you to succeed and I am not alone in this. If you pay attention, you will find a lot of people who are in your corner rooting for you. To succeed, you have to remember that this is not a leisure read. It is about taking action, and your first assignment is to flip to the next chapter. See you on the other side.

-James Williams

James W. Williams

PART ONE
THE BATTLE WITHIN

CHAPTER ONE
The Introvert's Bubble

"You never change your life until you step out of your comfort zone; change begins at the end of your comfort zone."
Roy T. Bennett

Living in Your Comfort Zone

We all have that space where we are the most authentic version of ourselves. In this space, there is no room for doubt, worry or fear. The world fades out the moment we enter this place and we experience a sense of calm. This place is known as our bubble and in this bubble, things happen effortlessly. The bubble is not always an actual place. It could be certain things or activities or even related to time. This calmness we experience within our bubble is not just random. And the things we have psychologically tagged as our comfort do not really give us the sense of calm that we think it does. For example, people whose comfort zone is linked to food might be inclined to think that the food is what makes them calm when in reality, they are simply projecting the emotions that they crave onto the food.

Your couch may be the space you have chosen as your comfort zone. Its cozy and plushy seats envelop you in a welcome embrace every time you sit on it. The proximity of the couch to all your favorite things like the TV, the coffee table which also houses your favorites snacks and books (and let's not forget, the remote) are just one of the many things that make it seem as though the couch gives you everything you need to feel emotionally comfortable. But the operational word here is "choose." You "chose" that couch. In essence, your comfort zone is a place of your choosing that feeds what psychologists refer to as an anxiety neutral position.

It is a very good feeling to be in your comfort zone but let me break down the actual cost of your "rent" if you choose to remain in your comfort zone. When your anxiety level is neutral or minimal, your stress level comes down and this is because you don't have to deal with any crisis, any uncertainty and you are obviously more in control. With the absence of these things, your performance level is steady. If a comparison was done between your performance level in your comfort zone and when you are out of it, there would be a startling difference. Imagine we have drawn up a line chart to show the differentiation between your performance levels in and out of your zone. Now let me describe what it would look like.

The lines from the "in zone" performance would be a perfectly straight line that doesn't deviate or fluctuate. The numbers would be below the radar but it holds steady. The lines from the "outside zone" performance would be the opposite. It would be on a wavering line that ascends and sometimes descends. The more you push past your comfort zone, the higher you ascend. I did say that the line sometimes ascends and descends but what is interesting is that no matter how low it descends, it does not get below the steady line that is your performance when you are in your comfort zone. What is the point of all this? Well, I will get to it in a second.

Introverts have a propensity to stick to their comfort zone. And this affects their ability to speak up in public. I know because I lived in one for years and it wasn't until I pushed past that zone that I got to discover some of the potential I have. However, I have also observed that introverts are not the only ones who operate from this place. A lot of people (possibly you included) are in a place in their life where they are just generally comfortable. Your current skills and talent are celebrated, you have a job or run a business that ensures all of your needs are taken care of and you are surrounded by the people you trust...so this begs the question, why would you need to take a risk at doing something that you are not really good at? The answer is change. I will discuss this extensively in subsequent chapters but let me put it into perspective here.

Change is one of those inevitable things in life. It will disrupt life in your comfort zone and if you are not prepared for it, you will be deeply affected by it. The only way to get ahead of change is to step out of your comfort zone and push past your limits. Since you are reading this book, I am pretty certain that the assignment that is taking you out of your zone is public speaking. This is the reason you are terrified. Not because you are terrible at it or you are worried that you would be terrible at it. You are just being pulled out of your comfort zone. Stop fighting it. Just take a deep breath and embrace the challenge. Today, you are leaving your comfort zone. Next challenge? Figuring out where the real battle is.

Public Speaking

The Fictional Friend or Foe

Back in high school, there was this girl I was so into. She was smart, incredibly beautiful and best of all, she was really nice to me. We took a few classes together where we sat and exchanged love gazes (and yes, this is a thing) all throughout. Our houses were on the same street so we sort of walked home together every day after school, which wasn't really far away. We didn't talk much, as I was painfully shy, but she seemed okay with it. She didn't say much either but she always looked at me with a smile. One day she didn't walk back home with me. I thought that was strange but then I saw her girlfriends, Leah and Sophie, waiting behind so I assumed they had one of those girlie events lined up. You can imagine my horror when I came to school the next day to hear the news that my Gina was dating quarterback "jerk face" Derek. I was shattered and heartbroken and listened to a lot of sad music for months.

That story I put up there was all in my head. Gina and I were never dating. Sure, we lived a few buildings apart—hence the walking home together part—but it was never really "together." She walked a few steps ahead with her friend and a cousin. Gina smiled generally at people because she was just a nice person naturally. And in truth, she probably only smiled at me once or twice. I just recorded it in my head and played it over and over again until it seemed as if she smiled at me all the time. Which leads me to the point I was trying to make. I made up that entire relationship in my head. I really liked Gina but there was no way I was going to talk to her, much less do anything about it. So, I created a fantasy relationship built on little snippets of reality and I actually ended up with real heartbreak for it.

Many of us make up this fictional battle in our minds and we react in fear to this make-believe battle we have going on. This is one of the main internal struggles we have when we are being called to speak in front of a crowd. Before we even get on stage, we imagine the reaction of the crowd. It doesn't matter if you are going to be speaking to your peers, a group of people you already share some similarity with or strangers. We picture that disapproving face in the crowd. We hear the mocking laughter and the crude jokes that are being made about us while we are even speaking. Sometimes, we even go as far as picturing an electrical malfunction that sets the podium on fire and sends the crowd into massive fits of laughter. The humiliation of all this cripples our courage and causes us to panic. But like me and my fantasy high school girlfriend, all of this is in our head.

The real battle is not facing the crowd of people who are hell-bent on your humiliation. The real enemy, in this case, is you. As humans, we have been gifted with an active imagination and this gift can be used in one of two ways. You can either use your imagination to fuel your dreams or empower your nightmare. In this case, you are using your imagination to force yourself back into your comfort zone, and we have already gone over what happens there. Some of you might say, "Oh, this happened to me in the past," but it is not happening to you right now, is it? No. You are just making up another excuse to justify your fears. The most powerful weapon in the arsenal of a public speaker is not their oratory skills or their great sense of style (although these are important too). It is not the absence of stage fright or their great people skills. It is their ability to harness the power of their imagination in their favor.

American athlete Michael Strahan is quoted as saying, *"We're our own worst enemy. You doubt yourself more than anybody ever will. If you can get past that, you can be successful."* I agree with him 100%. In the battle within, the enemy that we must face down is ourselves. Stop promoting theories that amplify your fears. Instead, make yourself your ally. This may require unlearning certain habits you have picked up over the years. A few pages down, you will get the full scoop on how to do this. For now, let us shift the focus from negative thoughts to finding positive reinforcements.

Finding the Right Connections

In a bid to get me to make more friends when I was younger, my mother invited her friends who had kids to come over. Either that or she would take me by hand to their houses for a visit. As expected, I was always reluctant. Not because the other kids were not nice or welcoming. It was just that being around them even made me more aware of my shyness, which worsened my anxiety. I never acted out or anything but my mother would always find me sitting by myself in one corner. She would sigh and say to me, "No man is an island, James; you need to be around people." I heard this phrase a lot as I grew older and at first, I thought it was all about just having people around you. Perhaps you could go as far as putting the "friend" label on some of these people.

I thought that our connections with people were mainly about our outward interaction with them until our dog, Jojo, died. Stay with me on this. I know I started with the sad kid on the playground and now you have the sad kid whose dog died. I have a point I am trying to make here. As you can imagine, Jojo's death affected me badly. I was sad for a long time and my mother encouraged me to write about my feelings in order to get through it. Reluctantly, I did. And I remember the words I wrote.

"Jojo never said a word to me. I did most of the talking and even then, he never gave any indication that he understood the words I said. But Jojo was my best friend in the world and we had a special connection..."

I wrote a lot of other things after that but it wasn't until a couple of years later when I was going through my stuff that this last sentence really hit me. Friendship is not about the people you have around you but about the connections that you make. No matter how much of a recluse we are, this is an important aspect of our nature; call it a biological programming that craves this connection. Some of us find it difficult to make those connections with human beings so we bestow it on either animals or inanimate objects.

James W. Williams

I know people who are deeply connected to their faith and a few who find this connection in their jobs. Why is this connection important and what does any of it have to do with public speaking? You see, the connections that you make in life have a way of bringing out the best, or sometimes the worst, in you. The deeper the connection, the greater the effect. Right now, I am not merely focusing on our connections with other people. I am looking at the things in our lives that influence our behaviors.

There is a lot of depth to this subject and I don't want to bore you with the details so I am just going to skim the surface and give you the low down on how this impacts your ability to speak in public. When we connect with something, we plug into it psychologically in a way that allows said thing to influence our thoughts and thus, our behavior. Take Jojo for instance. This dog brought out a side of me that not many people got to see. His antics, though frustrating at times, turned on the fun part of my brain and got me laughing like there was no tomorrow. Losing him affected my ability to turn that part on again.

Your paranoia about speaking in public can stem from the fact that you have absolutely no connection to anything that turns on that part of your brain. For me, my connection was activated by my love for my job as a salesman. That whole process where you meet a person, speak to them about the product or service that you are selling and then convince them to make a purchase was such a rush. I didn't identify public speaking with this connection I had with my job at first. When doing the research for my first public speaking assignment, I understood on a basic level that there was a link between making sales and public speaking. But when I personalized it by establishing that connection, it opened up a whole new universe for me.

What opens you up to people? What is that subject or topic that the second you start talking about it, you suddenly fall into a rhythm that is calm and comforting and you can ride that wave forever? Is it the work that you do? Or the people that you work with? How can you connect that with what you are about to speak publicly on? When you find the right connection, you will find your voice. And when you do find your voice, it is time to let that bird fly free.

James W. Williams

Taking Your Freedom in Leaps

So far, we have talked about three major internal issues that could impact your road to public speaking even before you set a foot on that part. These are deep-seated issues that may take months or years to change. This can give you pause and I understand why. We live in an age where everything is done rapidly. So it makes sense that we would want our transformation to happen overnight too. Well, let me burst your bubble right there. That is not going to happen. Not if you want a result that is sustainable throughout your years. Because this is not something that is exclusive to helping you become a better public speaker. If done right, it can help you become better at so many other things.

However, just because the process is going to take long does not mean that you should defer your public speaking assignment or goal until you think you are "fixed." Even if you have an assignment tomorrow, I urge you to follow through with it. It may not be your best performance but it will get you closer to your goal. The objective right now is to take things one step at a time. Before we move on to the next chapter, we are going to review the highlights of what we have talked about, and then you will also have a few simple tasks that you can carry out today to help nudge you in the right direction. These tasks are not one-off things that you simply cross off your to-do list. They help you build habits that will help you grow.

That said, here is what we have learned so far:

- Our comfort zone is where our performance level is at its lowest.
- Change is what spurs our growth.
- Self-doubt, more than anything, is what brings us down.
- The greatest tool in public speaking is one's imagination.
- To be a great speaker, you need to find your connection to what makes you want to speak in the first place.
- Transformation does not happen overnight. It starts with one deliberate step at a time.

Your tasks:

1. Say yes to an invite to a social event at least once every month.

2. Have a conversation with a perfect stranger every week (a few strings of sentences count).
3. Pick out five things or persons you have a connection with. They must be classified under the stuff you either like to talk about or who/what you like to talk about things to or with. Write out why and how they get you to talk.
4. Do a little research on some famous public speakers. Who do you identify with the most and why?
5. Include something very different in your routine today. Do that every other day, and you must not repeat these exercises.

CHAPTER TWO
CROWDED SPACES

"Wild animals run from the dangers they actually see and

once they have escaped them, worry no more.

We, however, are tormented alike by what is past and what is to come.

A number of our blessings do us harm,

for memory brings back the agony of fear

while foresight brings it on prematurely.

No one confines his unhappiness to the present."

Seneca

Social Anxiety 101

In the previous chapter, the primary focus was on the internal conflicts that impede our ability to speak in public. In this chapter, we are going to be looking at external factors that can stand in our way.

My aunt, who was a devout Catholic, was often fond of saying, "A sinner runneth when no man pursueth." Basically, some of the things that we fear the most are grounded in our imagination more than the existence of the actual thing or event that scares us. For people who suffer from social anxiety, the boogie man is often the crowd. And if you are going to move on to becoming an excellent public speaker, you are going to have to move past your fear of crowds. This is easier said than done and I know because I have been down that rabbit hole and let me tell you, it is not pretty. In order to defeat one's fear, you must first understand it.

In very succinct terms, social anxiety is a form of stress brought on by interacting with people socially. A lot of times, people confuse social anxiety with being shy. We all experience an unpleasant reaction when we are thrust into a social situation, especially if you are going to be meeting new people for the first time. It gets even worse if you are expected to speak to or address these new people that you are meeting. Our pulse becomes elevated, our palms sweaty and we experience this sinking feeling in our stomach. This is all perfectly natural. However, the difference between normal stress experienced when we are in those social conditions and social anxiety is that you can push through the normal stress. But social anxiety completely paralyzes you.

It is so intense that it has been classified as a mental disorder. So, if you find yourself unable to function in any way when you are in a social setting, chances are you are suffering from Social Anxiety Disorder and it is very important to see a doctor about it. Now, this recommendation does not mean that your dreams of public speaking are a foreclosed issue until your doctor says that you are better. I am saying that the first step to eliminating it is seeing a doctor. There are several reasons why people suffer from social anxiety and the degree to which they experience it can be influenced by a number of factors. For starters, there is a biological element to it. Having a relative who suffers from Social Anxiety Disorder increases your risk of having it. If you have a history of abuse, especially if this abuse started at an early age, your risk doubles.

In some cases, certain insecurities we have about ourselves can trigger an attack. If those insecurities are physical or visible, it gets even worse. It could be an ugly scar, a birthmark, or perhaps the sound of our voice. We feel that these attributes make us stand out in a very loud way and that people would not approve of this difference. So we anticipate their judgment and this puts us in an anxious state. For those who experience this intensely, they would rather not put themselves out there for that kind of judgment anyway.

Whatever the case, the road to recovery starts with acknowledging the existence of a problem and then taking an introspective journey that will take you to the root of the problem. For people who have gone through some kind of psychological trauma in the past, there may be a lot of unresolved emotional issues. Working with a trained psychologist can help you get to a place where you come to terms with what has happened and then release the burden of holding on to that memory. You may also need to undergo some behavioral therapy that would help retrain your instinctive reaction to certain situations. This way, your body does not have to go through the fight or flight response every time you are confronted with situations that trigger your memory.

People whose Social Anxiety Disorder stem from a biological proponent, like having the portion of their brain that controls fear function in hyper mode, may need medical treatment to get that under control. This again requires consultation with a doctor. Now if your anxiety is a result of some form of insecurity or low self-esteem, you can speak with psychologists to help you come to terms with who you are. And if it is something that can be fixed, it would not hurt to meet with someone who is qualified to do so. Just remember, they can only fix what is on the outside. I have seen cases where people had these insecurities about certain parts of their body, got it fixed perfectly, but they still battled with their insecurities. It becomes like that phantom limb that doctors talk about.

You cannot get to the point where you can comfortably speak publicly without first overcoming any form of social anxiety you may have. This is a delicate process that might open up some deep emotional wounds but healthy healing is what would follow afterward.

The Dreadful Cycle

Having looked at what social anxiety is, I want us to look at its impact on public speaking beyond the physical symptoms that we talked about. We have explored the *what* and touched a little bit on the *why*. Now we will go into the *how*. As a child, one of my favorite moments with my dad happened when we were in the garage together tinkering with stuff. It could be an engine, an electrical device or whatever my father got his hands on. The objective was to pull it apart, understand how each of the different pieces worked and then put it back together again. More often than not, the stuff that we put back together didn't quite function again the way it was designed to. It either got the "Williams Upgrade" or ended up making weird noises while doing what it was designed to do.

For us to successfully "upgrade" a device, we would have to thoroughly understand the role that each part had to play in the process and then figure out how it did what it did. Then we would have to break the cycle. It was either we took something out entirely or we took it out and replaced it with something better. When it comes to emotional trauma, I use the same approach. Anxiety, as with most emotions that happen in the extreme, go through a cycle. This cycle is made up of a series of events that take you from point A to point B and sometimes up to point D before bringing you right back to point A again. And then the process continues. The starting point for this cycle is the mind. There is no emotional angst we face today that does not first begin in the mind. There are external factors that can set things in motion but long before those things happened, the mind played its part.

When an event happens to you, the emotion you feel as a result—whether good or bad—is registered in your mind and identified with that event. That memory and the feeling that induced it is locked in your mind with certain markers that could be sight, sound or smell. This is why a specific scent can take you back to your childhood. Amazingly, this registered event does not have to be a firsthand experience. It is possible that you witnessed something that locked that event in your mind. It is also possible that you were told of an event that was so emotionally intense that it locked itself in your mind. And then you have the case where you made up an experience and somehow convinced your mind that it is a real possibility, that it also locks that false memory. I told you before—the mind is a very powerful tool.

Now that your mind has locked this memory, the next sequence in this cycle is the event that triggers the memory locked away in your mind. In this case, it is the crowd that you are trying to interact with. The crowd itself is not the problem. The problem is the way your brain interprets what it is seeing because your mind is feeding it information based on the memories unlocked. For social anxiety, the memory unlocked is usually linked to unhealthy relationships with people. Whether this memory is real or projected, if it is unpleasant, the brain interprets the social situation as a threat. When the brain senses a threat, it goes on alert and your natural preservation instincts kick in. Essentially, the signals being fed to your body are telling your impulses that you are not in a safe space and you need to get out of there.

These signals manifest as increased heart rate, problems breathing and muscles tensing up among other signs. These symptoms can amplify the information reaching your senses. An innocent laugh or smile at something general might seem as though it is targeted at you. A person walking towards you may seem like they are making a threatening advancement. This brings you back to your mind, where the whole process is put on repeat. All of these things happen very fast. The point when you walked into the room to the moment that you are virtually hyperventilating can happen in a matter of seconds. As the cycle repeats, the emotions experienced hit you like waves. Each one more intense than the last until the situation either escalates or you are removed from that moment completely.

For some people, the anxiety kicks in the moment they walk into a room full of crowded people. For others, getting on stage is what triggers the attack. Understanding the sequence listed here is key to creating solutions that will help you break free, and this is where we are going to next.

How to Break Even

In the first section of this chapter, I laid a lot of emphasis on the importance of consulting with a specialist to help get you over your social anxiety. That has not changed but that is just the first step. You need a doctor for many reasons, with the primary one being to get a proper diagnosis and possibly the root cause of the problem. Follow through on their treatment and management plan.

For people whose social anxiety falls within the mild to moderate spectrum, you may need to take a more proactive role in managing your anxiety problems. For starters, experts believe that what you have is related to performance anxiety. This is related to social anxiety but related to your performance than just being in a social setting. If this is the case, then this is good news. Performance anxiety, also known as stage fright, is very common and it is suffered by millions of people all over the world. You are not alone. As a matter of fact, your favorite public speakers suffered from performance anxiety at some point in their lives. One of my favorite examples is our country's most appreciated president, Abraham Lincoln.

Despite the rousing speech he gave at Cooper Union in New York, Abe was terrified of speaking in front of a large crowd. His fear was so great that he turned down an opportunity to speak at an event that would have taken his political career to the pinnacle. His note on the subject alluded to some anxiety issues. Of course, he went on to become one of America's greatest, but that required him stepping up to the challenge. Other famous speakers who had similar issues are Joel Olsten, Thomas Jefferson and even Warren Buffet—who was rumored to have been unable to get up and say his own name in class.

Now that we know who they are and how prolific they are at speaking, it is difficult to reconcile this image of them with the ones who were scared of speaking. But history paints a clear picture for

Public Speaking

us. But what speaks loudest to me is the fact that if they can overcome their performance anxiety, so can you.

To break the dreadful cycle of performance anxiety, you are going to have to first start with your mind, which controls all of the sequences in the cycle. The memories that trigger your emotions, which go on to activate certain impulses, need to be replaced. If you had a tragic stage experience, you cannot just forget that it never happened or delete it from memory. That is not how this works. However, you are going to have to take your focus away from those memories. Remember what I said earlier about the power of your imagination.

Darwin's experiment on the subject is a perfect illustration of this. He pressed his nose against a glass cage that held a poisonous adder within. When the snake struck at his nose from inside the cage, Darwin jumped back even though he knew that there was no way that the snake could get to him. In the same way, we are aware that the crowd we are about to speak to are not going to harm us. However, we instinctively react as though they would. So, stop seeing the crowd as your enemy and the stage as a kill zone. Instead, picture them as people who share your concerns and interests, because they do. If not, why else would they be coming to hear you speak? You have something to say that they would like to listen to so embrace the opportunity and just go ahead and say it.

I have mentioned a lot here in trying to explain the *how*. So I decided to simplify everything I have said in actionable points:

1. Stop running away. You need to face your fears head-on. It may require every ounce of discipline in you to do it the first time, but it gets easier over time.
2. Be prepared. There are very few people who can give great speeches at the drop of a hat. All those carefully and artfully delivered stage performances required hours of rehearsals, at least.
3. Focus more on your speech and less on the crowd. You cannot do anything about the crowd anyway.
4. Have more confidence in your abilities.
5. Be positive.

Get Ahead and Be Heard

It is said that when Thomas Jefferson spoke during his public speeches (he gave only two of them throughout his eight-year tenure), he spoke in very low tones that required you to strain your ears before you could hear him. Mahatma Gandhi was the same way too. But they did not let their voices get drowned in the sea of people they had to surround themselves with. What they did instead was keep their words concise but very effective. Not everyone has the gift of gab, however, when it comes to public speaking, it is better to keep your message succinct yet impactful than to drone on endlessly.

As we go further into this book, we will learn the very art of public speaking itself, but not before overcoming the fear of speaking in public. Also, if you are going to wait for a time when you no longer get anxious about speaking before actually doing it, you are never going to do it. This is because those jittery feelings caused by anxiety never really go away. It has been almost a decade since my first speaking assignment but I still get sweaty and shaky right before I go in front of the crowd. And I have been a public speaker on more than fifty occasions. The only difference is that the fear is not as paralyzing as it used to be. You just have to embrace the fear, don't let it envelop you. Put your feet down and tell yourself that today, you are doing this.

And on that note, here is a summary of what this chapter has been about:

- Social Anxiety Disorder is a mental disorder brought on by the stress of being in a crowd. Performance anxiety is a form of social anxiety associated with stage fright or speaking in front of a crowd.
- Social anxiety is very common but it is treatable, manageable and very possible to overcome.
- The messages that you feed your mind will determine your reaction in a social situation. If you feed yourself messages linked to fear, you will react in fear.
- Deferring your public speaking to a later date when you might feel more comfortable will only prolong your torment. It is better to bite the proverbial bullet now.

Your tasks:

1. Speak to a doctor about your anxiety. You may not get a fix for it right away but the knowledge that you are doing something about it can be very reassuring.

2. Take up the habit of meditating at least thirty minutes a day. This practice will teach you how to get your body to relax even when you are under pressure.
3. Find a mantra that you can repeatedly say to calm yourself in stressful situations. It could be a phrase, words of affirmation or confidence boosters. I like "Hakuna Matata."
4. Every morning, look at yourself in the mirror and give yourself a compliment. It might feel awkward at first but that feeling passes in time.
5. Maintain longer eye contact with people. For strangers across the room, a three-second gaze is fine. For people you are having a conversation with, try as much as possible to maintain eye contact. Don't glare. Don't stare.

Maintaining eye contact helps you build confidence in your social interaction skills, and we will get into more on confidence-building in the next chapter.

CHAPTER THREE
BUILDING BLOCKS OF CONFIDENCE

"Wouldn't it be wonderful
if you fell so deeply in love with yourself
that you would do just about anything
if you knew it would make you happy?
This is precisely how much life loves you
and wants you to nurture yourself.
The deeper you love yourself,
the more the universe would affirm your worth.
Then you can enjoy a lifelong love affair
that brings you the richest fulfillment from inside out."

Alan Cohen

The Lies We Tell Ourselves

Growing up, we were taught to see the wrong in telling lies to other people. There was always honor in telling the truth. The reason that was given to us most of the time was that it made it difficult for people to trust you if you had a habit of telling lies. Lying is a self-preserving trait and this is not something you are trained to do. It just comes to you naturally. This is why a three-year-old would tell a bald-faced lie. The main objective of lying is to give a narrative that serves our purposes and interests best. If lying becomes a habit, then it becomes a serious problem and there could be some psychological angle to that. Lying is so complicated because it never really just ends with one lie. It grows from one tiny untruth in a giant entangled web of lies that entraps the person telling the lies and I find this very interesting because when lying is involved, it is not just the person lied to that is affected.

As a matter of fact, lies affect the person who told the lie even more. And I am not referring to the late-night visit from karma that most people believe delivers judgment to those who have erred on the wrong side of humanity. I am talking about the impact on the psyche of the person perpetrating the lies. If you have ever been on the other end of the stick, you would know how much it hurts to realize that you have been lied to. In other words, when a lie is being told, both the person lying and the one being lied to end up getting really hurt. This hurt may not surface right away. In fact, you may even realize that you have been lied to but on some instinctual level, you sense it and that causes the hurt to linger and fester, leading to a very precarious relationship at best. Knowing all of this, I would like you to ponder on the next question I am going to ask. What happens when the person being lied to and the person telling the lies are one and the same person?

There are lies we feed ourselves and sadly, not many of us were prepared for the consequences of this. The bigger problem with the lies that we tell ourselves is that the lies are usually not anything grand. They are small pieces of information that we assimilate in small doses over a long period of time. In other words, we do it without even realizing what we are doing. Sometimes, the lies are a reflection of what society tells us. We are tagged by culture, status, race and even gender. We then wear these labels and let it define our potential. When your ability to perform is characterized by the label that you wear, you will face a more internal struggle in your bid to succeed. Some people may argue that labels help give you a better understanding of yourself. I agree with those people, but to an extent. You see, unless you are the one giving yourself the label, instead of just adopting the one placed on you by society, you will always end up shortchanging yourself. What do I mean by this?

Let us assume that your parents have tagged you as "painfully shy." They saw certain traits and behaviors that you exhibited when you were much younger and then identified it with shyness. From that point onward, this is the information they reinforced. If they were meeting with friends and you hesitated to socialize, they would immediately apologize and then emphasize the message, "We are sorry, but our boy is incredibly shy." You probably heard this a lot in social settings and you internalized the message. As you grew older, you personalized that message. Your excuse for the awkwardness you experience when you socialize is excused by your "shyness." Your acceptance of this message is so wholesome that you characterize everything that you do with the label. So, when the opportunity comes for you to speak in front of your peers, without giving much thought to what it entails, you play the label tag and wriggle your way out of it.

Lies like these act as a barrier to your growth. Abraham Lincoln's excuse was that there was an illness that ran in his family that prevented him from speaking in public. Imagine what would have happened if Abe just threw his hands up and embraced the limitations set on him by this illness. He would probably have lived a regular life without anything out of the ordinary setting him apart from the men in his era. But we are privileged to know what he evolved to become and it is impossible to picture Abraham Lincoln as anyone less than the phenomenal person he was. The lies that we tell ourselves only serves to amplify our fears and increase doubt in our abilities. Telling yourself that you cannot speak in public is only there to protect yourself from the possibility of failure if you attempt to. It is you telling yourself that you are not qualified for the task. Let us look at the implications of this.

Life in Rocky Places

Have you ever seen a flower blooming on a plant that is growing through rocks? It is incredibly beautiful and at the same time mind-boggling. I look at it as a miracle because under normal circumstances, that plant is not meant to be there. For a plant to grow, it needs soil, light and water. Rocks have very limited amounts of those which is why you don't see plants thriving in such places. But then you have extraordinary situations like these where nature decides to defy the odds. The plant in question did not just grow out of a rocky spot. It thrived, bloomed and became a thing of beauty that is admired. As exceptional as this story is, the main message is that nothing is impossible if you put your mind to it.

I don't know the kind of environment you were born and groomed into. It could have been a rocky spot that did not offer the essentials you needed to thrive. Either that or your environment was a rich and fertile soil that offered you everything that you needed to succeed in life. Whatever the case, here is one glaring truth: Neither of these environments listed can cause you to fail or succeed in life. The only thing they can do is either make it harder to succeed or harder to fail. And this is because the key ingredient that determines how far you go in life is what you feed yourself with. And this brings us back to the lies that we tell ourselves. Imagine the kind of conversation that plant must have had with itself in that dark, dry and lifeless place where it took root as seed. It must have heard the message that only plants in fertile soil can grow. The rocks must have told it to give up because there was very little sun and water that came through. Still, the plant did not internalize those messages even though they accurately reflected the reality of the situation on the outside. To thrive, it would have had to look inward for resources to draw on. I believe that if the plant looked inward and found the same hardness on the outside reflected inside, it would have folded up and died.

But it didn't. Instead, it found an oasis on the inside that made it resilient to the external dry conditions. The growth may have been slower than that of its peers but the moment it broke through to the surface, that process sped up. At this point, the outside world began to conform to what was already on the inside and the result was a flower that was as distinguished as a piece of stunning art. Let us bring it back to your present-day dilemma with public speaking. If you want to unleash the potential on the inside of you, you need to stop paying attention to what you are being fed by your environment. Maybe you are looking at your inexperience on the proposed topic, your supposed shy nature, your speech problem and so on as the things that limit your ability to succeed. Focusing on these things automatically places parameters on what you can achieve and how far you can go. Instead, focus on your goal.

Make it your business to manage your conscious mind (aka your inside voice) and remind yourself that you can achieve the success that you desire in public speaking. Those other issues we talked about might slow down your process or make it that much harder for you but the determining factor at the end of the day is you.

Building Pillars with Stones

We all have our respective struggles in life. Some of us are very good at disguising our pain. Others wear their hearts on their sleeves. Whatever category you belong to, recognize that the struggle is real. However, also remind yourself that your success is equally real. You may have had to deal with social anxiety, stage fright, poor self-esteem and lack of faith in your abilities to get to that spot where you can comfortably speak from. Whether this is your first time or thousandth time, there are hurdles that you have had to or will have to overcome in order to make your mark. The purpose of this chapter is to guide you to that place where these hurdles can become the foundation on which you build your claim to success.

Now that you are aware that you are at the helm of your affairs and not necessarily a victim of some biological or psychological factor, you cannot afford to sit on the sidelines. You will need to make conscious efforts to first let go of some "truths" that you have believed in. Broaden your horizon with your mind. I have a piece of painting in my home that I consider to be one of my most valuable purchases and this is not because of the amount of money I had to put down for it. It is what it symbolizes to me. The artist in question is an Indian man who was born without any function in his arms. Using his feet and mouth, he is able to create such incredible art. Every time I look at the painting, I am reminded of the possibilities.

Possibilities are not always born from the availability of what you need to succeed. It is birthed at the point when you make up your mind to follow through on achieving your goals despite the stones that life has thrown at you. At that point, instead of letting your weaknesses cripple you, you let them inspire you to be greater. When your fears and doubts are screaming the loudest and telling you that you can't, you turn up your voice in your head and yell back that you can. The moment you can do this, your success script is born.

Regaining and Retaining Your Crown

If at this point you are unable to tell yourself that you can do this, I would suggest you stop reading further and go back to the beginning of this book and start all over. I am not saying that your fears would have disappeared or that you have zero doubts about yourself. Because they will always be there. And if for some reason you have no fears or doubts, I would say you should go back and read chapter one because it definitely sounds like you are back in your comfort zone. At this point, you should still feel some pressure about the next step that you are about to take but at the same time, you should be able to say that you can do this.

Reclaim your crown by positively affirming your abilities and keep the crown thereby tuning out the voices of doubt. There are no pills that can get you to this point. And there is no amount of time spent on the psychologist's couch that can fix this. This is a choice that you have to make 100%

on your own. All the things I have said here can only inspire you to take that next step but without you actually taking that step, you are always going to be on the other side of the line. We have one more hurdle to cross before going to the next part where we actually start preparing for public speaking. But it requires you to admit to yourself that you can do it. Still, need a little push to get you closer to the line?

Here is a recap of what we have learned so far:

- The words that you tell yourself have a more powerful effect than anything anyone else can say to you. You need to start "watering" yourself from the inside with positive words.
- The only reason you cannot speak publicly is that you have told yourself that you cannot.
- Nothing is impossible the moment you put your mind to it.
- You control the limits of your potential. You can only perform as good as you think you can perform.

- Positive affirmation is one way you can take the challenges that life tosses your way to build your success.

Your tasks:

1. Picture yourself performing on stage. From start to finish, let the entire experience be positive. Meditate on this image at least once a week.
2. Write out in detail how you would like to see your performance as a public speaker. Place this written article somewhere accessible and read it out loud every day. Modify it as you grow.
3. Think back on your life and find an experience that sees you overcoming a challenge. It does not have to be anything grand. If you have been following through on the tasks assigned to you in the previous chapter, you should have something on your list. If not, get to it.
4. Ask three people in your circle who know you on some level to list out your qualities and your "weaknesses" on two separate sheets. Study that list and figure out how to play them up in helping you achieve your goal. Don't internalize the perceived

weaknesses; instead, empower yourself with them. For instance, if someone says that you are withdrawn in crowds, rephrase that to mean that you like to observe your environment.
5. List three qualities that you have and how you think those qualities have served you in your job, in your relationships, and in life generally.

The final chapter in this section reflects on the journey we have taken so far and puts us in a mental headspace that challenges what we have accepted as the status quo. We enter into the minds of champions and find out what makes them tick.

CHAPTER FOUR
ELIMINATING OBSTACLES

> *"The biggest obstacle you will ever have to overcome is your mind. If you can overcome that, you can overcome anything."*
> **Unknown**

Emotional Roadblocks

This quote here brings to mind a quote that I heard from an unlikely hero. I am one of those adults who enjoy kiddie's entertainment. You can say that at heart, I am still very much a big kid. Some of my favorite heroes are not from Marvel or DC Comics. They reside in either Dream-Works or Pixar animation studio and right now, the guys from *Kung Fu Panda* are the best. In the latest series, there was a part where one of the characters tells his students "before the battle of the fist comes the battle of the mind." I can attempt to set the premise for this statement but that would lead to a whole different book and we both know that you didn't sign up for that. Besides, given the title of this subject, I think we already have more than a fair idea of where I want to go with this. But hold that thought for a moment. Let us leave the kids arena and step into a wrestling or boxing arena.

Have you noticed that before a fight (I am not a big fan of those by the way, but it makes for an excellent illustration), the people fighting against each other are put in the same room in front of a small audience where they get to talk smack to each other? For the event organizers, it is a great way to promote the show and make good sales. For the audience and anyone watching, it is great entertainment and an incentive to watch the fight. For the fighters, their objective is different. Somewhat sinister, some may say. For them, this smack talk is a way to get inside their opponent's head and throw them off their game. Before the battle of the fist comes the battle of the mind.

Now let us bring this back to you. Going on stage is where your "battle" will happen, but the fight begins long before you step onto that stage. And as I am sure you probably know by now, the person you are fighting against is you and that is usually the toughest fight because you know all of your emotional weak spots, and so when you get into a "smack talk" session against yourself, you knock yourself out before you step into the ring. A typical smack talk between two people usually targets each other's weaknesses. What happens in a smackdown is that you have these two parties making fun of things are sometimes very personal to the opposing team. Now in your situation, you are not making fun of yourself (although some of us use humor to criticize ourselves), however, you are doing a very good job of undermining your abilities. Say for instance you have an issue with the way you pronounce certain words; when you are having that internal smack talk with yourself, every insult or negative comment you have ever received concerning this flaw is amplified and made the center focus. This becomes worse when you are put in a situation that requires you to use this thing that people have made fun of you for before even getting yourself ready to go on stage.

In general, every insecurity that you have ever faced will get its time in the spotlight and in the game of minds, this would make you even less confident and less willing to go on the offensive. It would seem as though you are putting yourself out there for other people to judge when in reality, the only person doing the judging is you. These negative comments are able to weigh on you because of your emotional connection to them. To help you overcome your emotional hurdle, I decided to take cues from the king of smack talk since we are on the subject. If you are a fan of trash TV, you may have come across something called "Yo Mama." It is a form of smack talk where people make dumb jokes about their opponent starting with "Yo mama." I used to think that there was no strategy to it and that it was all about having the best punch lines. But I was wrong. Imagine this. You have a situation where one person is confronted with a personal jab that is made into a joke and everyone laughs because it's a very good joke. And then the person at the receiving end of that joke doesn't take it personally but instead, they turn it around and make a comeback with it, sometimes knocking out their competition in the process.

Then you have the other person who hears this joke made about something that makes them feel insecure and they feel crushed by it. In this situation, they are unable to see past the intention of the other person and so they get out of the game earlier than they should. The difference between the two of them is not just in how they reacted to the jokes made about their insecurities. It is how they heard the joke. The first person saw an opportunity in those insults, and they used it to get their comeback, whereas the second person didn't. It is the same thing when you are having a mental smack talk with yourself. You need to detach yourself emotionally from whatever you are holding against yourself. Look for a loophole in it and then make yourself come back with it.

With the new information you have just received, let us go back to the hypothetical insecurity you are having with the way you talk. Chances are, you are worried that when you get on stage, your speech defect would become obvious. Rather than talking yourself out of the game, think of it as an opportunity to educate the people around you on the problems of speech defect. What this kind of thinking does for you is it helps you recognize those things you consider as flaws and accept them. And don't just accept it as a weakness. Look at how you can make it your strength. In this hypothetical scenario, your strength would be a firsthand knowledge about something a lot of people are ignorant about. By taking this perspective, the stage no longer becomes an arena to showcase your weakness. Instead, it becomes a platform that would frame your strength. I guess what I am trying to say in all of this is that first of all, you need to embrace your flaws. That is the first emotional battle you need to overcome. If you embrace your flaws, no one can use them against you; not even yourself.

Criticism and the Critic

When it comes to criticism, I feel like the art world is the best place to use as an illustration because artists are faced with a lot of criticism for the work that they do and yet, they somehow exceed the expectations of their critics and excel in their game. An example of one such artist is the great Pablo Picasso. When Picasso first showcased his art technique to the world, he received a lot of backlash for it. Some people even went as far as describing him as demonic and his drawings as something otherworldly. Many of those people didn't think he would make it far in the art world. But he did and today's generation references him as probably one of the greatest. And his critics? Well, let's just say their claim to fame is the words that they used to describe his art, which doesn't reflect well on their legacy at all.

When you are confronted with an opportunity to speak in public, the second emotional hurdle you would have to overcome is criticism. In this regard, first, we have ourselves to blame as we are own worst critics. And then you have criticism from second parties. But in my opinion, the criticism from second parties is not really important at this point because what they say is usually an echo of what you think. Besides, there are constructive forms of criticism that build you up. So, this brings us back to you. It is your responsibility to stop yourself from falling into the trap of critics. You have to get to the point where you understand that this is not about you or your performance. You are not getting on stage to be judged even though it feels like it. Standing in front of a group of strangers feels as though you are opening up yourself for those on the other side to criticize but this is far from the truth. You have to change the perspective on this if you want to get past the problem of criticism. People who come to hear you talk are there to take something away from what you say and the only time they will criticize is when you get on there and don't say anything. Even at that, you would still find people who would consider your silence a very vocal statement.

The bottom line is that you can't control what people are going to think about you and so why would you want to waste your mental resources on what might or might not be said? If someone like Pablo Picasso, whose art is highly sought after today, could get criticized for his work, I would say that we are all fair game. So, for this segment my advice is this: Rather than stay preoccupied with the opinions of other people, focus on your craft. Focus on what it is you are going to say (we will get into that in subsequent chapters). This is how you overcome the hurdles associated with criticism. Now I know this is not easy and this is exactly why I used the art world as an illustration. In art, perfection exists but perfection is based on perspective. You have heard the saying one man's meat is another man's poison? There will always be opposing views on everything. It doesn't matter how good you are, there will still be people who won't value what you do. Even the person that is rated as the best public speaker in the world would still have a sect of people who would think that they are worth nothing. In conclusion, accept the fact that some people are not going to like you anyway, however, you are not getting on stage to be liked. Focus on your objective and when the criticisms come after you are done, remember the lessons from the previous segment and roll with the punches.

The Power of Imagination

There was something I learned very early in life and this is thanks to the relationship I had with my parents. They instilled in me an appreciation of this fundamental truth and I have taken this truth with me in everything that I do. It is very simple, really, and I am sure that at some point in your life, you may have heard it. The truth is this: You are a product of your imagination. In order words, if you can think it, you can be it. If you cannot think it, you cannot be it. It doesn't matter how educated you are. It doesn't matter how connected you are. You can only be as powerful as your imagination. If there is anything I have tried to establish from the beginning of this chapter up to this point, it is the fact that the mind is where nearly everything you experience is created. If you are going to imagine negative things, you should expect to have negative experiences. If all you can picture at this point in time after everything you have learned so far is how you are going to go on stage and be terrible at it, my dear friend, it is guaranteed that you are going to be terrible.

This is how influential your imagination is. Now if you picture yourself getting on stage and doing excellently well, chances are this is going to be a reality for you. However, your work does not stop at imagining the results. There has to be some work that goes into ensuring that what you envision becomes a reality, and that is what the rest of this book is about. I want to get you to that point where you're completely psyched about being on stage. Don't focus on rating your performance (at least not until after you are done). All that can do for you is to slow you down. The idea of using your imagination to fuel your performance is not about getting 100% on your score sheet or the applause that you get. It is about getting on the stage and enjoying the experience. When you enjoy the experience, it doesn't really matter what other people think about your performance. Now if you combine your expectation for your experience with the practical preparatory guidelines which we will get to later in this book, you increase the odds that people are going to enjoy seeing you stand on stage this way. So far, everything I have talked about has had to do with the reorientation of your mind. I want you to get into the space where you have the winner's mentality. So, here is what you should take away from this segment: You don't have to have the best punch lines. People just need to see that you are up there and having a good time, and you start that process by picturing yourself there.

Satisfying Your Fears

Staying in line with the theme for this chapter, there are a few questions I want you to ask yourself. Questions like what is the worst thing that can happen to you on stage? What is the craziest, most insanely, out of this world thing that can happen to you on stage to ruin your public speaking experience? The sooner you can find the answers to these questions, the faster you can move past your fears. The concept of satisfying your fears is not about focusing on the negatives. The fact is that oftentimes, the things we fear the most are the things that we have not really thought through. It is like the boogeyman. We have this vague notion of this entity and we don't confront this vague notion. Instead, we just accept the reality of its existence. But then when you actually face it head-on, you realize that there wasn't any reason to be afraid in the first place.

This is what it means to satisfy your fears. Ask yourself those questions you are not comfortable with and ensure that you get the answers. Are you afraid that when you get on stage the light is going to fall down on you? Or maybe you fear that your clothes are just somehow going to magically disappear? These sound like silly questions, but you will be surprised by how these silly questions shape our fears. So, today, right now, take a sheet of paper and ask yourself what exactly are you afraid of and do your best to be honest with the answers because it is from the answers that you get the solution. When your fears are satisfied, they lose their hold over you and when they no longer have a hold over you, you become free. And in this case, you are free to be the best public speaker you can be.

This chapter was about helping make sense of the emotional struggles you have and giving you a little insight into the consequences of your thoughts because yes, the things that you think about can shape your experiences. In this recap, we are going to focus on the four major emotional obstacles we face and how we can push past them:

- You undermine your abilities by focusing on your weaknesses. To win on stage, you must first win the battle of the mind. Embrace your flaws.

- Your fear of criticism can get the better of you. Keep your focus on your efforts instead of trying to predict the opinions of others.
- Your expectations for your performance on stage sets the tone for everything. Expect great things.
- Fears have a paralytic effect. Free yourself by confronting those fears.

Your tasks:

1. Write a vivid description of what you imagine your stage experience would be like. There are only two rules for this. The first rule is that you don't limit yourself in any way. No matter how silly you think a concept might be, if you want it to be a part of your stage experience, include it. An example would be you imagine that your hair on stage would be perfect as that of a movie star. It doesn't matter if you have hair or not, just include it as part of the experience. The second rule is that no form of negativity is allowed. You cannot include any negative element in this narrative of your stage experience.

2. Make a list of all the possible things you think can go wrong on stage. This list should be written in a question and answer format. So, instead of imagining what you think will go wrong, ask yourself a question about it. For example, instead of saying "I am worried that the lights will go off," ask yourself, "Why would the lights go off when I'm on stage?" And then you try as much as possible to answer those questions. After you are done compiling Q and A, the next step would be to evaluate these fears.
3. Look at the questions and then deliberate on them. Decide on if a fear (phrased here as a question) is in the same category as the boogeyman or if it falls within the realm of possibility. Beside each question, write down your conclusion on the subject. If you think it's valid, indicate that. If not, write the word *irrational* beside it. This will help you sort your fears into categories.
4. Read through this list every single day leading up to the day you have to get on stage.
5. For the questions that you feel are valid, create an action plan on resolving them.

PART TWO
SETTING THE STAGE

CHAPTER FIVE
UNDERSTANDING THE WHYS

"Your preparation for the real world is not in the answers you've learned, but in the questions you've learned how to ask yourself."
Bill Watterson

Find Your Purpose

Now that we have pushed past some of the internal struggles you are having, it is time to start asking the tougher questions and taking a tougher stand on things. Before this chapter, I would say that we have been taking baby steps to lay the foundation for the next stage. And now, this is the point where you ask yourself questions like, "Why are you doing this, anyway?" There is a huge difference between wanting to do something and understanding why you have to do that thing. And that difference is the motivating factor that will get you through the stormiest parts of this journey. We know that life will always come with challenges and with this topic, I am not only referring to public speaking. This is something that applies to every area of your life as well.

The crazy thing about these challenges, in my opinion, is that they are not meant to derail you or take you off the path you think you are supposed to be on. As a matter of fact, I think they are meant to propel you forward because the challenges you go through in life is what helps you define the reason why you are even doing it in the first place. Now let us bring this back to public speaking. I find it hard to believe that you're going up on stage to just check one item off your bucket list. In theory, it might be a cool idea, but why did it even make it on your list anyway? That question is for you to answer if that is your situation. For every other person, I would say that any reason that does not resonate deeply within you is not enough to keep you going, especially when the challenges come (I guarantee that they will). If you understand why you have to do something, even though this is not exactly something you liked in the first place, you stay motivated to do that thing.

I remember when I was a very young lad, my father was very involved in a community project that helped young people get jobs. There was a weekly event that he was in charge of and he used to have me tag along with him. I hated it because we had to wake up early to get to where we were going to in order to get the resources that we needed to use later in the day for this weekly event. This was a big challenge because these locations were on opposite ends of the city. On one end, you had the resources and then at the other end, you had the event. And my dad only had this day of the week to do it because he had to work full-time every other day. I, for the most part, hated it and you can't blame me—I didn't understand why I had to be involved in it anyway. It is not like my dad and I had any special bonding moments during the course of it (or so I thought). I always looked at it as something my father wanted to do and it didn't help that my mother called it my father's pet in that down-the-nose way only mothers can. But despite the challenges associated with pulling each weekly event off, I never saw it slow my father down in any way. He never missed a week and he was, as far as I can remember, always on time. It was almost as if with every single challenge, he was more inspired to do it. On the morning of one of those event days, he woke me up and as usual I grumbled and complained. Then I got it into my head to ask him this pertinent question: "Why don't you ever get tired?" His response was simple but very profound. He said, "Because of Tim and every other Tim that is out there."

Now the Tim story comes with a lot of emotional baggage for my family, especially my dad, so I am not going to go into that here. However, I remember his response because his vivid description of his purpose immediately got me to understand why my father remained dogged about his work. I bet every time he had to drag himself out of his bed on a day that he should have been resting, the mental image of Tim would flash through his mind and he would be up in a flash. Public speaking is not something you should do for clout or to impress some people. Not unless you are okay doing it that one time. But if you want to make a life out of this and go far, if you really want to surmount the challenges ahead, you have to understand why you were doing it and when you understand the *why*, the challenges in front of you are not going to be enough to stop you.

Moving with the Crowd

Before I get into this segment properly, I would like to comment on how many contradictions there are in life. On one end, you have people who tell you that it is important for you to be an individual. They say don't roll with the crowd. And then on the other end, you have people who say the voice of the people is the voice of God so when the crowd speaks, you just have to listen and go with. It is hard to discern what applies best in this scenario, especially if you are still struggling with a lot of personal issues within yourself. If you haven't defined yourself and you still get into that place where you do not appreciate the value that you have to offer to the world, it is hard to decide if you are going to stand by yourself or just blend into the crowd.

When you are going for public speaking, this is one of those cases where we need to apply a little bit of both—and by both, I am referring to your individuality and the opinions of the crowd. The fact is this: People are coming to hear you talk and when hard-working people take the time out of their day to come and listen to you, chances are there is a message they are hoping to get out of what you say to them. Now, I don't know what platform you are going to be doing this public speaking thing on; maybe it is a work project or perhaps you want to hone in your skills at being the master of ceremonies at events. It could be something as simple as making a best man speech at your friend's wedding or maybe something a little more complex like your first foray into the political field...whatever your reasons are, you have to bear in mind that the crowd is there for a reason and if you are unable to carry them along in your message, you will lose them.

That said, I also don't believe that you should pander towards everything that the crowd wants. I have a background in marketing as you probably know, and there is something I learned from my mentor in the field which is very key in executing a successful marketing campaign. We are taught that oftentimes, the customer doesn't know what they want. At least not until you pitch it to them. I feel like it would make sense to apply that wisdom here. Your crowd may be coming to your event with one thing in mind, but there is a way you can pitch your individuality to them that would get them to become interested. So now you see why I say you have to toe the line between having a little bit of your individuality on display and catering to the needs of the crowd. In subsequent chapters, we will look at how you can move the crowd but before we get to that point, this is where you lay the foundation by focusing on how you want to get the message across using the two essential ingredients for public speaking: your individuality and the people's need.

The Truth Vs Your Truth

After deciding on how you want to pass the message across, the next important thing is to focus on what the message is going to be about. You know how they say that there are two sides to every story? In the same way, when it comes to public speaking, there are multiple perspectives. However, until you understand the complexities of this, there are two perspectives that matter the most. The first one is the truth. It is always important that when you get on stage, no matter how unpleasant it is, you much share that truth for what it is. If not for any reason, do it for the sake of your integrity. When you go on stage and speak in front of a crowd that is a bell that cannot be un-rung, you have to ensure that every word that you put out there is supported by the truth. If you are trying to find the courage to speak the truth, you must first start with the assumption that the people you are talking to are going to be very intelligent. If you have paid any attention to political debates, you would see that candidates come well-prepared with facts and figures.

People are not just going to come to the event and swallow everything that you say hook, line and sinker. You have people who are going to take notes, people who are going to analyze everything that you have said and most likely they would want to implement it in their own lives. Now if parts of what you have said or everything that you have said is untrue, you jeopardize their chances of success and undermine your own integrity. This is not a track record you want to set for yourself. In the news, we have heard of who has made an income of selling lies to the public— and some of them have been very successful at it too—but at the end of the day, their lies caught up with them. Then on the other spectrum, you have people who have maintained their integrity in the trade and still amassed a fortune in the process. That said, our objective here is not the wealth that comes from playing in the field. In general, it is said that a good name is better than riches. This speaking opportunity you have been given would put you on a platform that can elevate you to a global stage. It will bring opportunities that will transform your life. A lot of changes will happen but the one thing that should not change is the integrity associated with your name. And this brings me to the second perspective: your truth.

Now in the application of the truth that you're going to share with the crowd, I am very sure that there are personal lessons you learned along the way. As a public speaker for whatever purpose, it is important that you infuse these personal experiences with the truth that is either already out there or that you just discovered along the way. This gives you authenticity and if you are true enough to your person, it will connect you better with your crowd. Please pay attention here, as this is a big deal. Most people may not want to identify with the truth that you put out there but if you stay in that truth and you are authentic in it, you would be able to sieve through the crowd of wanderers to find the exact kind of crowd who you want to share your ideas with. People think that having a large crowd is a testament of your success as a public speaker but in reality, it is the number of people in that crowd who you are able to impact successfully that speak to your achievements. And I believe that the kind of people that would fall in that category are those who connect with you. They are the ones who would be keen on implementing those ideas that you share. So, in conclusion, stay on course with the truth and by all means maintain your authenticity in sharing that truth.

Define Yourself

Have you ever sat alone in the dark and asked yourself, "Who am I? Why am I here? What is my purpose?" I think at some point in our lives, we have all had what the world describes today as an *existential crisis*. In this state, we question virtually everything about us. This is good. Except that when you are having an existential crisis, you are not exactly operating from the right frame of mind. So, the answers that tend to come up stem from fear, anxiety and sometimes loss. To answer the question of who you are, you need to step away from the circumstance. Because, if you let yourself be defined by the circumstance surrounding you, you would fail to achieve your full potential. There is so much more to you than your experiences and if I know anything about life, it is the fact that experiences change according to the state of your mind. This is why certain things that caused you so much pain some years ago can be laughed at when you look back on them now. So if your experiences are going to define you, it means that you are essentially whatever you are experiencing at a specific point in life. This would be very sad because it would mean that there is a chance that we are described by a sum total of our failures, our successes, our shame, and our glories.

This is not how I picture each person. I feel that we have a lot more to offer. And as a public speaker who is bent on speaking the truth and only their own truth, you need the strength of character in order to pull that off. Strength of character comes from being rooted in the true version of yourself. You can only be the true version of yourself if you take the time to reflect on these questions that we asked at the beginning of this segment and provide answers that are outside whatever experiences you are having at the moment. This may be a lot to ask, but in the task segment of this chapter, I have given a detailed step-by-step process on how you can define yourself.

Remember, confidence doesn't come from knowing all the answers or being liked by everyone. Confidence comes from knowing the right answer to the question of: Who are you? Answer this question and there is no stage that would be too big or too small for you.

To wrap up this chapter, let us go over the highlights:

- Connect yourself with public speaking by having a clear understanding of why you are doing it. It doesn't have to be something grand. But let it be vivid enough to get you off the couch and onto the stage anytime you are called.
- The winning combination for winning the crowd over is saying what they want to hear and doing that the way that only you can.
- Maintain your integrity by speaking the truth. Showcase your individuality by being authentic.
- Define your personality and then use this personality to connect with people.

Your tasks:

1. Start by identifying your passions. Write out a list of things that you would be more

than happy to do even if you were not getting paid for it. Set this list aside.
2. Make another list of things that you wish you could do and you feel that if you did them it would make you happy.
3. Create an action plan on how you can do those things and give yourself two weeks to follow through on this action plan.
4. At the two-week mark, look at the things you have checked off this list and the things that you haven't. The things you have done, write out how they made you feel. The things that you haven't, write out why you didn't follow through on them.
5. Now sort the things that you have done that you actually enjoyed and would love to progress on, and add them to the first list that you created for this task. For the things you haven't done, file that under a "curiosity" folder.

The answers that you arrive at will provide clues to your personality. They may not be related to public speaking yet but as you continue to grow this list, you get a better knowledge about yourself. When you know yourself better, you develop a healthier relationship with yourself and it is from here that you can confidently answer the questions of why, what and who. In the next chapter, we are going to take the focus away from you and put it on the subject that you plan to speak on. Brace yourself!

CHAPTER SIX
CHOOSING YOUR FIGHTS CAREFULLY

"Choose your battles wisely. After all, life isn't measured

by how many times you stood up to fight.

It's not winning battles that makes you happy,

but it's how many times you turned away and chose

to look into a better direction.

Life is too short to spend it on warring.

Fight only the most, most, most important ones, let the rest go."

C. JoyBell C.

How to Decide on the What

Before we go any further into this topic, it is important that we acknowledge the journey that you have taken so far. Double up on the accolades if you have been following through on all of the tasks given in each chapter. By appreciating how far you have come, you are able to mentally empower yourself for the journey ahead. And even though you feel as if you have regressed in certain areas and have not quite gotten over your fears, don't let that deter you. As for fear, I don't know if you have heard this being said, but I will go ahead and share this with you. Courage isn't the absence of fear but the choice to go ahead and do what needs to be done anyway. In other words, *that* fear is always going to be there. The only difference is that over time, it will become easier to overcome. From the moment you are invited to speak until the second you get off the stage, you will experience that jittery feeling that makes it seem as though your legs have become jelly and your stomach is sinking. But with each speaking engagement, you become even more experienced at ignoring them. With that assurance, let us tackle our next task for the day.

Now, this particular chapter is another very important step in this journey because this is where you get to decide on what you are going to verbally put out there on stage. People underestimate the amount of work that goes into preparing for a speech. When we see our favorite public speakers do their thing on stage, because of their excellent elocution and smoothness in delivery, many of us (myself included) assume that this is something that comes naturally to them. But the truth is the best speeches are well-thought-out and rehearsed days, if not months, in advance. I don't know of many people who go on stage and "wing it," as they say. Not unless you are a professional and even the professionals take that time to practice. Earlier on, we used political debates as an illustration, and I am going back to it again because I feel like this is the most brutal form of public speaking and if you can get it right here, you can get it right with everything else.

When you look at political debates, you see these candidates arguing their points with each other, but what you don't get to see is what happens behind the scenes. Before the date for the actual debate, there are several reenactments of the debate and the goal is to get the candidate to that point where they can speak comfortably about possible issues that might be brought up. They want to be able to argue their points while ensuring that their opinions get heard. The people coaching them through these mock debates emphasize the importance of sticking with the facts while showcasing their personality. You may not be going for a political debate but if you want to excel as a public speaker, you have to imbibe the same practices. Take your time to plan your speech and then rehearse it as often as you can.

Chances are, you have already been given a topic to work with. If that is the case, the best way to lay a foundation for an interesting speech is by conducting thorough research on the topic. Remember, integrity is important, therefore it is essential that the truth is infused in your narration of the topic. The next step would be to combine the facts that you now know with your experience. In a situation where you have not been given a topic but just a general theme, what you want to go for, or rather, the first question to ask yourself is, "What would I like to talk about?" In making your decision, you have to bear in mind that whatever topic you choose must stay in line with the theme of the event. In formal settings, keep your topic on issues relevant to the kind of organization hosting the event. For informal occasions, you may want to update your speech to include trendy news relevant to the occasion. Then you have to figure out how you can align this thing you're talking about with the theme. I recommend that you start out by focusing on your area of expertise. You will always have firsthand knowledge on the subject and information that is most likely not common knowledge for your audience.

Pay Attention to the Seasons

I am fairly certain that you know that I am not referring to the weather. The world that we live in today is a very sensitive place. There are so many social issues that have risen up to the surface that the level of political correctness one must master will make you feel like you are walking around on eggshells or worse, an emotional minefield where a single verbal faux pas can cause a catastrophic backlash with enormous repercussions. In sticking with the truth, you also have to be sensitive to the social consciousness of your environment emotionally and mentally. And even if you are speaking at a place where you feel the social consciousness is behind the times, you have to remind yourself that with the presence of technology, it has torn down the walls that once separated nations. News travels at the speed of "now." You may be speaking to a local audience without realizing that you have been put on a global stage. You do not want to go viral for the wrong reasons. Now I know that this may feel like added pressure but instead of looking at it that way, think of it as a way to make you even more equipped for your speech.

Your awareness of the seasons would give you a better connection to the people in your audience. The fact is, times have changed...a lot. People are thinking and feeling things a lot differently than they used to in the previous centuries. I know that throughout this chapter and in the chapters leading up to this point, I have and will continue to emphasize on sticking to the truth for the sake of integrity. But my focus on this segment is to open you up to the real nature of the truth, especially in these modern times. We have heard it said quite often that truth is a bitter pill to swallow. This is true and delivering the naked truth on certain occasions will not get you any extra points. Rather, it can set you up for total failure, which is not good, especially if you want to make a living off public speaking. So, how do you navigate this murky terrain and come out without a smudge to your name?

First of all, you must have a good understanding of the times that you are in. The issue of gender, sexuality and equality should be factored into the truth that you are telling. You cannot carry on the same narrative of the past and expect the present to comply. Secondly, you must realize that the truth is not finite. There are different perspectives on the same subject and the truth depends on the view where you are taking your standpoint on. So, ensure that you factor in as many perspectives as possible in the narration of your truth. What I am trying to say is that you need to be delicate when you deliver your truth. Be empathetic to the people and the emotional atmosphere of your environment. Say, for instance, you are delivering a topic that is related to a science project. Factor in the views of some people who may be concerned about the potential damage that this science project can cause the environment. Come up with a view that would still deliver on the truth and facts of what you want to talk about, but at the same time make an attempt to address the concerns raised by other parties. It is imperative that your speech is inclusive. Use your voice in telling the truth (remember the part about being authentic) but try as much as possible to avoid statements that would make certain parties feel excluded. Because if you fail to do so, not only will your speech be interpreted as offensive, you also put a cap on the growth potential for your target audience. The fine art of developing the kind of speech that can be appreciated in today's climate can be compared to that of the performance artist who has to walk a tightrope across a long distance while juggling as many objects as possible at the same time. It is difficult, but it can be done.

One thing I feel I must warn you about is being guarded about becoming too politically correct that you lose the ability to make any impact with the platform you are standing on. Some experts hire professionals to do the speech writing for them and then they have another team who would go over it and accede to the contents of the speech. If you can afford to have this many people on your payroll, this is a genius solution. If not, my rule for this is very simple. I try to answer these two questions correctly:

1. Am I trying too hard to be liked than I am trying to share practical solutions?
2. Is this courting controversy or putting too much airbrush on the truth?

The best place to be in answering this question is somewhere in between.

Creating a Winning Strategy

You have to remember that the goal here is to win. And when I say win, I am not referring to a medal of honor that would be given at the end of the stage because there isn't one. Neither is it to get off each stage with the loudest applause (although it would be totally cool if that happened too). The goal is to overcome your fears, get up there on stage, hold the crowd in your sway (even if it is for all of five minutes) and then get off the stage knowing that you have accomplished all four and can do it all over again if you are called to do so. I would say that we have gotten the first part locked down. Those tiny insecurities whispering reasons why you can't and shouldn't must be silenced and replaced with the voices telling you that you can. Among those voices, your voice must be the loudest. Arm yourself with daily affirmations designed to fire you up from the inside for the tasks ahead. Choose words that resonate deeply with you. At first, it may sound a little unusual coming from you. To get myself comfortable with positive affirmations, I started up by listening to or watching videos of my favorite celebrities doing their Monday morning motivation speech. There are some that are so upbeat that you suddenly feel like a lion at the end of it. Look for what works for you and roll with it.

The strategy for getting up on stage is simple. Just do it. The second your name is called up on stage, don't freeze and certainly don't think about it. Just get on there and every single thing that you have been practicing will come to you. You may even surprise yourself with a few tricks that you had no idea you knew. To hold your crowd in sway, think of yourself as the magician and your speech as the act. You must have the killer introduction, several parts that are clearly broken down to take your audience from one point to another and then the grand exit.

Let us start with your introduction. Some public speakers like to start off with humor (we talk about this a few chapters from now) and some like to start with very dramatic facts. I have known speakers who start off with a compressed biography on themselves. Choose the one that you are most comfortable doing. Humor does not have to be of the same quality as what you would expect on Comedy Central, but it should be able to tease a smile out of them. Unless you have perfected the art of comedic timing, I would not recommend going for those classic jokes where you pause for the crowd to laugh. I made that faux pas once and there was dead silence. However, I was prepared for that too. After a second or two of no laughs, I simply went on to say, "What a tough crowd. Obviously, no one came here for the jokes so I will just get right into it." This elicited some small laughs and I just moved on. Now, I make it a routine. I give a dead joke and then make some fun about nobody laughing and just get into speaking. If you are going for dramatic facts, start off by stating statistics that are not related to the subject you are discussing and are not commonly sourced for. Even if they are, you can switch up your perspective by interpreting those statistics in relatable terms. So, instead of saying "Out of 100 million people, only 10 million people brush their teeth at night," you can try saying "Out of the ten people sitting close around you, possibly only one went to bed with fresh breath." This immediately brings their focus to the topic and stirs up a personal interest in the subject.

If what I have talked about seems a little too dramatic for you, it is okay to just start with a very, very short biography about yourself. It can be just three sentences and if it was written down in a book, it shouldn't exceed three lines. Also, remember that your introduction should match the theme of the occasion. The next should be the subject matter of the speech. Don't give a long drawn out statement that you read word for word. Divide it into segments and discuss on each point. You can have little notes and cue cards containing major points. If your presentation is being done with a projector and screen for your audience to look at, even better. List out your speech in bullet points on the screen and throw in an image every now and then. It keeps them visually engaged. At the six to ten minutes mark (it depends on the duration of the speaking event for me), I throw in some humor. I like to use funny cartoons or images that look odd, hilarious and out of place and when the crowd laughs or snickers, I chime in a fake "oops" and then tie it into the rest of the presentation. I try to finish ahead of time so that I can ask questions (if the event allows) and I usually have small souvenirs with me. Any audience member with the right answer gets a souvenir instantly. It is a fun way to keep my people entertained and gives me better vibes when I get off the stage. Find a routine that will work for you, practice it and nail it.

Bracing Yourself for Conflict

The statement "expect the worst and hope for the best" used to be something that scared the life out of me. I don't want to expect the worst. I want only the good things to happen to me. My sentiment towards this statement is even amplified when I think of public speaking. But this was before my experience with public speaking. After my first successful stage debut (you read about my earlier disaster), I realized that the more prepared I was, the better my experience on stage. This was all fun and good until I had a Q and A segment added to one of my public speaking events. This was while I still working at the marketing firm. I was not ready to field the kind of questions that came at me that day on the stage. It felt like it was a personal attack. Most of the questions were from disgruntled employees who felt that I was now representing the company since I was speaking for them on stage. It was, of course, unfair of them to attack me that way but in hindsight, if I had come on to the stage better equipped, I would have been able to field those questions in a better and more appropriate way.

It doesn't matter how nice, warm, creative or inspiring you are, there are still people who will come at you with questions that will throw you off your game. You cannot prevent that by attempting to be even nicer, warmer, more creative or more inspiring than you already are. The only way to combat it is by anticipating the resistance thereby anticipating their questions and preparing your answers beforehand. Try as much as possible not to take some of these questions personal, as the resistance is not always directed at you. In some cases, the people in the audience may have some preconceived notion about you and in receiving your message, they filter it through the lens of that notion they have about you and respond in that manner. In some other cases, perhaps, the problem has more to do with the message than it does with your person.

Whatever the case, don't try to explain their actions. Instead, do your best to bring the focus back to the message that you are trying to get across. And in the event you are asked a question that you absolutely have no idea how to respond to, you can either deflect or admit to not knowing. The problem with deflecting is that you could miss out on a learning opportunity for both yourself and the person who asked the question. And I would only recommend deflection in cases where the question asked is inciteful and hateful. But if it comes from a place of genuine curiosity, you could tell the person that the question that they asked is very intriguing and that you would love to have the time to explore that train of thought even more. Go a step further by asking them to reach out to you via your professional email address so that you can share your findings with them. Chances are, with a response like this, you would win over more people to your "fan base." In a situation where the conflict is not expressed at the venue, you will find some people going online to express their displeasure. Again, do not take it personally. If it is not harming your reputation, I urge you not to give it a second thought. If there were constructive criticisms made, look at them carefully and learn from them. This is a learning process for you. Try as much as possible to learn, adapt and evolve.

After completing this chapter, I arrived at a not-so-startling conclusion. You cannot please everybody no matter how hard you try. The best you can do is to ensure that you please the majority and that majority should include yourself, the organizers of the event you will be speaking at and a larger part of the audience. If you can do this, you should be fine. That said, let us look at how I arrived at this conclusion based on the lessons from this chapter:

- In deciding on what to speak on, you have to ensure that the topic, whether given or chosen, is the truth wrapped around the theme of the event or vice versa.
- Be sensitive to the emotional climate and guard your words diligently.
- Have a strategic plan that would take you from the point of your stage fright to the point where you exit the stage. Use affirmations, speech plans and stage presence in building a winning stage routine.
- There will always be something negative that certain people will say. Recognize that the goal is not to be liked by everyone but to deliver excellently in your public speaking.

Your tasks:

Do these tasks before any public event:

1. Identify the nature of the event you will be speaking at. Get specific details.
2. Find out as many details as you can about the kind of people that would be coming

for the event. Information like age, gender, ethnicity and so on will play a key role.
3. Relate the details from one and two with your expertise and your experience.
4. Brainstorm on at least five different topics that fit all the information listed above and draft your speech around them. The more prepared you are, the lesser the chance that you would be taken off-guard.
5. Practice your speech for at least two hours every day leading up to the event.

CHAPTER SEVEN
LOOKING THE PART

"All fashion brands are about looking good. Being Human is also about doing good. And you can do good by the simple act of slipping into a t-shirt or a pair of jeans."
Salman Khan

Addressing Your Dressing

When you get on stage to talk in front of the crowd, you get just the one chance to impress and you know what they say about first impressions lasting longest. Your window to create an impression is only about ten seconds (this is for a very generous crowd) and if you get it wrong, in the minds of your audience, you might end up spending the rest of your speech trying to make up for that poor impression (if that is even possible). It doesn't matter how intelligent, smart or articulate you are. It doesn't even matter if your speech was written by the great Steven Spielberg himself. There is very little you can say in ten seconds or less that would instantly impress your audience. However, you are aware of the saying that a picture is worth a thousand words, right? Well, your dressing can speak several volumes about your personality and what people can expect to hear from you.

Now, I am going to try and get you to be comfortable with this topic because I feel like a lot of introverts have this mentality that putting effort into your dressing, especially when it is not even something you are comfortable in, is somewhat pretentious. I know this because, like most introverts, I am more comfortable in my own skin (and by my own skin, I mean my favorite t-shirt from college paired with cargo pants and a pair of multi-colored socks). But seeing as the world does not qualify this as classy, it is hard for me to feel comfortable when I am dressed in anything but my comfy wear. To come to terms with this, I had to learn some hard truths about dressing. One of them is the fact that comfort makes you feel good but it does not in any way mean confidence. And my objective when I get on stage is to exude confidence and to achieve this, it was important that I understood that comfort is for my comfort zone and confidence is for the stage.

Confidence is the currency that buys you the "consideration" of your audience so if you really want your speech to make a lasting impact, you cannot afford to wear the regular flip-flops, t-shirt and jeans. However, this doesn't mean that decking yourself in designer duds from your head to your toes is going to score you major points either. Especially if the designer gear is not put together in a way that makes it visually appealing. You would be amazed by how your appearance can distract people from the beautiful message you are trying to get across. So, before you head off to the nearest clothing store, the first thing you need to do is to start with the basics. Start with what you like to wear. I already know that the jean and t-shirt look is a classic favorite but it comes off as super casual, and even if you are speaking at an informal event, it still wouldn't make sense. Not unless you do an upgrade on the look you generally prefer. An upgrade does not necessarily mean a big budget or total discomfort.

The reason I vote for going with an upgrade of what you like to wear is that it gives you the comfort that you crave while at the same time giving your audience a better representation of yourself. So, what exactly does an upgrade look like? Let us assume that your favorite outfit combo is a pair of denim jeans and a t-shirt. The upgrade for this is totally doable regardless of your gender, age or the type of event. There are two looks you can aim for with this. The business casual vibe for that casual affair and then the complete professional look for that formal event. First, for the semi-casual or business casual look, let us start with your jeans. They must be fitted and in a dark shade to nail the business casual look. Anything less than this would take you farther away from the look. Pair with a button-up shirt and a jacket in a color that contrasts nicely with your jeans. Both must be fitted too. To complete the look, wear formal shoes. This would mean court shoes for the ladies and the derby, brogues or oxford for the gents. The shoes should be in a shade of black, brown or navy. For the head to toe professional look, gents can throw in a tie and ladies should keep the color combinations white, black and blue. Do not try to pull off the monochrome look with denim. It rarely ever works. This is one of those times that you should play it safe.

If you want to ditch the denim look entirely but still keep things within that comfort range, swap your jeans for khakis or slacks. Today's design options have found a way to get your slacks to transition between an active lifestyle and formal wear effortlessly. There are so many options. At the end of this chapter, you should be able to decide on what the best possible look for you would be and how you can avoid making a terrible fashion statement on stage.

Style Mistakes to Avoid

Welcome to Style 101 for public speakers. If you consider yourself a fashion guru, don't skip to the next chapter just yet. I may have one or two fashion tips that will go on to improve your stage experience. We have established that while the streets may be your daily runway, the podium where you do your public speaking is anything but that; as you will come to learn eventually. It is where your performance as a public speaker will be judged. If the information you put across with your outfit does not match what you are trying to say, you can be certain that most of what you say will not be heard. And now I know I said earlier that we should pay less attention to what people think about us. However, this doesn't mean that you should arm them with the tools with which they can use to judge you. That said, here are a few fashions don'ts for a public speaker.

1. Thou shall not show skin

The stage is not the platform for you to showcase skin in any way and this is not a gender-based type of instruction. It goes for everyone. The only thing that should be showcased is your talent and your wit. So ditch those cargo pants, shorts and any type of shoe that will reveal your toes. For ladies, your dress or skirt should be below your knees. Now, this is not a backdated 1940s instruction. It serves a very practical purpose. There is a possibility that the podium you will be standing on to deliver your speech might be very high. A very short skirt would give the people sitting down at least a few feet from you an unexpected view that neither you nor they bargained for. In my opinion, it is better to wear an outfit that prevents this than to deal with the outcome afterward.

2. Thou shall not dress casually

It doesn't matter if the event you are speaking at is being held at a beachfront in Hawaii. The rules of engagement remain the same. The best you can do is to tie in the theme of the event into your outfit to ensure that you do not stand out terribly and look like you are not "playing with the team." This is what accessories are there for. You can stick with the basics with your main outfit and then use a few accessories like ties, scarfs or hats (if the occasion calls for it) to expand on the details.

3. Thou shall not be insensitive

You can make a statement with what you wear. That is why they call it a fashion statement. And now more than ever, it is important that you pay attention to the kind of statement that you are making. For instance, getting on stage wearing a mink fur coat is a loud statement to animal lovers that you don't care about the pain and suffering that animals have to go through for your outfit to be made. Not only that, it is quite distasteful. You may not share the same sentiments with animal lovers but you shouldn't have to throw it out there in their faces, especially not on a platform that is as public as this either.

4. Thou shall avoid bold colors and loud patterns

I am of the opinion that it is very hard to put on bold colors and loud patterns without looking like a clown and I am sure that there are a lot of people who would agree with me. There are certain colors that do not belong on stage or in front of the public unless you are going on stage as an actor in full regalia. For a more professional feel, it is best to stick to muted colors, as they help to tone down your personality. Another thing that muted colors can do for you is to prevent a situation where your outfit distracts your audience from what you are trying to tell them. Muted colors are colors that fall within the white, black, dark blue, brown and grey spectrum.

5. Thou shall not go on stage in a rumpled outfit

If you would rather do your laundry, do not skip out on ironing your clothes. They make you appear shoddy, disorganized and irresponsible. Remember what I said earlier about letting your clothes speak for you. Don't take any chances with the perception you want your audience to have about you.

How to Dress Like a Pro

Now that we are done with the list of don'ts, it is time to focus on the dos. Essentially, if you want to look the part of a public speaker, these are the things you need to do to get you started:

1. Pay attention to your grooming

There is nothing wrong with sporting a beard; not even a long one at that. But you have to keep them clean and trim. The caveman chic look was a great look for Shaggy from *Scooby-Doo* but it is more likely to get you mentally booed off the stage. Ladies, this is not the time to put glitter on your eyes and amp the color volume in your makeup or hair. Keep it simple yet elegant. Most nudes will go well for the occasion. If you are feeling daring, try a pop of red on your lips.

2. Give hygiene your 100%

It is odd that I am talking about hygiene since I think I am addressing a group of adults. Nevertheless, it must be done. Have a shower before you go anywhere on stage. Brush your teeth and do the flossing too. Use a nice deodorant and don't forget to trim your nails. Your outfit for the speaking event should also receive the same treatment. You would be amazed by the difference something as simple as this can do for your whole look.

3. Go easy on the accessories

Accessories are meant to accentuate your look. They bring it together and give it an overall finished look if they are done right. Bold statement pieces like jewelry look great on the gram and can get you on a centerfold spread of a fashion magazine but they do not belong on a stage when you are speaking. Go for simple understated pieces that have an elegant look.

Also, do not try to wear more than one accessory at a time. It makes your outfit "busy" and in fashion speak, that is not something that you want anyone to use in describing your look. Finally, if you want to follow the fashion trend, that is great but go for one trend at a time. If all of this sounds a little too complicated for you, just keep it simple. My general rule is until you are able to hire a professional stylist, stick with the fashion basics. It is hard to go wrong with that.

4. Dress for the occasion

We already established that public speakers should go for the semi-casual or purely formal look and then integrate certain pieces into their attire to tie into the event. But when I say dress for the occasion now, I am focusing on the theme of your speech. For instance, if you are going to give a speech relating to success in a specific field, it is important that you look the part. People should be able to look at you and get the success vibe off of you. I remember coming across a viral image of a young man who was giving a YouTube lecture on how to get 1 million views for your videos when he only had videos with a little under 600 views. I think the irony of it is what made the poor guy famous. If you are going to reach success, you must look the part. Now I must emphasize here that success does not necessarily mean that you have to rock designer outfits from your head to toes even if you can afford it. You would make better use of your money if you combine the pieces that make up your total outfit in a well-coordinated manner.

5. Infuse your personality into your style

With the list of dos and don'ts provided here, it is easy to lose yourself in the process and end up looking like a factory-made version of other public speakers. Having your own style in the mix helps you stand out from the crowd and also makes it feel more comfortable being on stage. Just because you want to be perceived a certain way shouldn't mean that your personality should be muted.

Complete the Look With a Good Finish

Most fashion magazines would tell you that you need great accessories to complete a look. As we have already talked about this, what else could I have to say on the subject? Fashion is more than just the clothes you wear. It matters how you wear them. You can get all the clothing tips from the best stylists in the world and have the best designers do their best work on your outfit but at the end of the day, if you fail to wear it right, you could end up giving the wrong kind of impression. And to wear it right in this business, you need to nail your posture. You can improve people's perception of yourself with the way you stand, sit or gesticulate.

Your competence in certain circles is determined to an extent by how you carry yourself, and this may seem unfair especially since you know that you are probably one of the few people who can do what you do excellently. But again, it is that mind translation thing. People are prone to judging a book by its cover and despite the numerous warnings that preach against this, the societal standard for assessing a person's capabilities is based on the first impression. This emphasizes the need to pay more attention to not just the way you dress but to how you wear your outfit as well.

To project confidence and competence, you need to maintain an upright position. Keep your head up and for men, ensure that your chest is not closed in. Dragging your feet on the floor when you move connotes laziness while unnecessary gesticulations can make you seem more nervous than you actually are. You may not feel confident about your performance on stage but there is no reason to see this. If they do, they may not have confidence in what you have to share with them. Recognize that you have important information that could potentially make a difference in their lives and it is your obligation to ensure that you do not give them any reason to question the validity of what you are trying to say.

So, after complying with the basic fashion principles and compiling an excellent speech, the next thing to do is to walk the talk...literally. Let your walk exude the confidence that you need to make it work.

Fashion is more than the clothes that you wear and it is essential in establishing yourself in the minds of people. You can use it to your advantage or set yourself up for failure with it. I vote for using it to our advantage and I am sure that you would agree with me too. That said, let us look at the main points from this chapter:

- Comfort and confidence are two different things. You dress for comfort at home but dressing for confidence is what you

should aspire to when it comes to your stage style.
- Make a statement with your fashion but it is important that you are making the right statement for your brand.
- There are general rules in fashion to help you keep your look stylish and socially acceptable. However, your style is also an expression of your personality. Don't forget to include that in your overall dressing.
- The wrong posture can give a wrong perception about your competency and confidence. Ensure that you master the right posture.

Your tasks:

The primary objective is to help you define your stage style and to do this, you need to complete the following tasks:

1. Do a current assessment of your closet and using the pointers in this chapter, determine what outfits you feel would be stage-worthy and put them in a separate pile.

2. Create a "look book" consisting of stylish outfits that you strongly admire. You could keep your focus on public speakers or expand your search to include actors, legal professionals or any person whose formal style strongly matches what you aspire for.
3. Using the look book, evaluate the pile of clothes you have selected in step one and try to get them to match the various looks you have selected.
4. If what you have does not match the looks you want to create, make a shopping list to accommodate what you need.
5. Continue to build on what you are working with. Most importantly, every other year or so, switch things up. While there is nothing wrong with sticking with the same style if it works for you, you can quickly get stuck in a comfort zone. Be a little adventurous but don't go overboard with it.

PART THREE
GOING FOR GOLD

CHAPTER EIGHT
THE ART OF PUBLIC SPEAKING

"You are not here to merely make a living. You are here in order to enable the world to live more amply with greater vision with a finer spirit of hope and achievement. You are here to enrich the world and you impoverish yourself if you forget this errand."
Woodrow Wilson

Qualities of a Good Public Speaker

There is a public speaker who is most suitable for a specific situation but then there are distinct qualities that put you in the same league as the big guys. It is not by the number of Instagram followers that you have or the number of events you are able to book annually, or even by the amount people spend to book you for an event. Those are the perks that come with building a solid brand for yourself and requires the right combination of publicity, hard work, consistency and possession of certain qualities that I will be discussing very soon. These distinguishing qualities are sometimes innate talent that is built on over time with training and practice. However, it is very possible for you to move from where you are right now to become good in your craft by honing in on the following skills:

1. Connecting with your audience

All of your tasks and training right up to this point would not serve you well if you are unable to connect with your audience. They are the reason you are on that stage in the first place. To connect with your audience, you have to first understand that being there is not about you even though they have come to hear you speak. It is about them. You are the speaker but rather than segueing into a long, drawn-out monologue, you have the responsibility of making it seem like a dialogue without the other parties doing it. In the next segment of this chapter, I give a detailed breakdown of this quality and a short example to help you get started. It may not immediately turn you into a crowd whisperer, as the charm switch that you need to turn on is unique to each crowd. Still, we will cover the basics to help you do more than just get by.

2. Being a master storyteller

In every chapter of this book, I shared a little story about myself and found a way to tie it in with the theme of that chapter. This is not because I am a person who just loves to share stories about myself. This is a deliberate attempt to:

a) Stop you from being bored
b) Make the concept more relatable to you
c) Prove that this is not something that was lifted off some other person's page but an actual experience

Storytelling humanizes your idea and paints a picture that your listener or audience might find more conceivable. You may have the best theories and the greatest solution for a problem in this century but if you cannot get people to understand it, it will always remain a theory. A good public speaker must master this. So, when you share, create or look for a story that best illustrates your ideas.

3. Voice modulations

Before you continue reading, take a minute to read a few sentences of this book out loud in a slow voice without any inflections. Disregard the commas and any other punctuation marks. If possible, record this on your phone. You will observe that you sound uninteresting and if you keep at this for at least twenty minutes, your own voice would have a snooze-inducing effect on you. In a crowd, this effect is multiplied and you don't want that. Voice modulations help you build on the two points listed above. You are able to give your speech a semblance of a conversation which is essential to keeping your audience engaged. Master this and your storytelling will take on a new dimension. Think of the narrators in a movie. The emotional inflections in their voices help you connect with the story even though you don't see them.

Charming Your Audience

A public speaker shares their ideas with an audience. A good public speaker shares their ideas with an audience and holds them in their sway. There are so many distractions in today's world. The advent of the mobile phone makes it that much more difficult to compete against them for the attention of your audience. There are simple strategies you can employ to get and sustain the attention of the crowd, whether it is a small presentation with a handful of people or a stage delivery with a large crowd.

1. Come with a message that would surprise your audience

The Internet provides a wealth of information and there is a very strong possibility that a significant number of the people in your audience may have more than an average idea of the topic you want to discuss. If you stick to the general information, you might end up feeding them with the same boring stuff and that kind of recycled information can earn you a few minutes of their time. After that, you may have a tough time regaining their attention.

2. Use a language that they understand

You want to impress your audience and I get it. But don't use bogus words that sound impressive without the ability to convey the true meaning of the words or the message you want to get across. For instance, the word I want to use in describing the true state of your audience if you choose to use big words in your speech is *discombobulated*. But don't you think it sounds a lot better and keeps you on track with this article if I replaced that word with *confused* instead? Stringing a few sentences together using big words could make it difficult for people to follow your train of thought, and even if they manage to scale through the first few minutes of your speech, there is no guarantee that they would keep this up throughout. Stick to simple and easy-to-understand words.

3. Get off the stage

Just because you have been set up on a podium shouldn't mean that your movement is restricted to that space. The entire room is your stage and as long as the movement does not interfere with the audio, there is no reason you can't do your thing from where the crowd is. This makes you seem accessible and when people feel this way about you, they become more open to your ideas. And when people are more open to whatever it is that you have to tell them, they pay more attention. It is really that simple.

4. Be flexible

For a novice public speaker, I can understand why you would want to create a script for your performance and stick to it. But if you observe several yawns a few minutes into your speech, it may not be working for your crowd. In this case, you may have to flip the script. If you were too upbeat, you may have to tone it down a little bit. If you are taking it slow, you may have to increase the tempo. And in some cases, you may have to veer completely off course (we talk about this in the next segment) and get the crowd buzzing in excitement before you bring them to the topic in focus.

Showing Your Witty Side

You do not have to be a comedian to get your audience rolling in laughter. And while it would be great to hear that glorious sound, the objective for public speakers is to inject some excitement into the room and in so doing, keep your audience engaged. For someone who is just overcoming their natural tendencies to be shy, it is a very daunting prospect to get on stage and amuse a crowd. From my personal experience, you can get the crowd moving by doing nothing more than being yourself. You have different options on using your wit to create a humorous moment. I am going to list a few ways you can do this. Go with what comes naturally to you. In fact, with practice, you may even discover a technique that I did not include on this list and this is one of the things that makes the remarkable journey you have embarked on that much more interesting.

1. Tell a story

We all have that embarrassing tale that we have lived through. Narrating that experience with a few exaggerated details can turn out hilarious. Sample this story with a small crowd and observe their reaction. If it is what you hoped for, embellish it a little and tell your audience. Be sure to include every funny detail you can recall into the narrative. However, it is important that you pay attention to the kind of crowd you are sharing this story with. An audience from your workplace who are there to witness a presentation where you pitch your ideas to them might not appreciate a joke about your escapades at the club. To avoid a situation where you might offend a race, gender or religious belief, it is safer to stick with narratives that are self-deprecating.

2. Give an activity that your audience can carry out

This may not immediately cause anyone to go into a laughing fit but at least it would get your audience moving. However, only do this if the crowd is not much and if you feel that the energy levels are dropping. From my personal experience, this works very well during training. I split my crowd into teams and come up with group bonding activities that pits them against each other. The competition gets them fired up.

Public Speaking

For a small crowd of people who are just meeting each other for the first time, at the start of the session, I ask everyone to fill out a card and drop it in a box. The instructions on the card ask them to tell two truths and a lie about themselves. About twenty minutes into a one-hour session, I pick three random cards, call out the names, read the contents of the card and then ask the audience to guess the truths and the lie. This takes about five minutes and then we get back to the session. It creates an atmosphere of familiarity and eases the tension in the room.

3. Tell a joke

Now, this right here requires timing, gesticulating and timing (again) to get the desired results from your audience. You might hear the same joke from three different people and have three different reactions to the joke and this is because of how the joke is told. Sure, when the same joke is told over and over again by the same person, it loses its humor. But when some other person does it and with flair too, you find yourself laughing even if you know exactly how the story ends. The key is the technique. You have to know when to smile, when to wriggle the eyebrows, where to screech and where to throw in the punch line. To successfully pull this off, you need to practice your joke. For those of us who find it difficult to get through our own jokes without first laughing our heads off, this bit might be difficult. However, if you have a knack for this sort of thing, this might be the best weapon in your arsenal.

Elocution

I think that this builds on the point I made earlier about using a language that your audience would understand. The emphasis, in this case, is on more than just the use of big words. The objective is to ensure that you are able to communicate concisely and clearly to your audience. So, matters like the clear enunciation of your words, the variance of your voice pitch, and the use of body language are thoroughly examined.

Enunciation: This is your ability to speak clearly and pronounce words in a manner that is understood by your audience. For people with speech defects like having a lisp or stuttering, there are speech therapies designed to help you navigate the difficulties associated with your condition. I, for one, am of the opinion that there is nothing that can stand in the way of you attaining your dreams. With hard work, commitment and consistency, you can turn your biggest disadvantages into a platform that sets you up for the future that you desire. If English is not your native language and you are speaking to an audience that is comprised mainly of English speakers, a speech training class might help you with the enunciation. Make friends with your dictionary. Learn new words every day and practice the proper tenses where those words apply.

Pitch variation: To maintain a certain mood in your crowd, your voice decibel must not rise or fall below a certain level. If you go above, you start to appear as though you are screaming the words at your audience. That may work if you use it on a particular word to create emphasis about something you want to illustrate. Use it sparingly and even then, you have to time its use properly. If your voice note dips too low, you become inaudible to your audience. Maintain this note for too long and you might as well pick up a violin and play a slow accompanying tune that would lull your audience into a deep sleep. At the same time, keeping the same pitch throughout your speech can quickly become monotonous. This could instigate the same sleep-inducing phenomenon as keeping your voice too low.

Body language: Your facial expressions, as well as the movement of your body parts, can clue people in on the state of your mind. Without saying a word, your facial features and body language can tell anyone if you are frightened, excited or just plain bored. If the words that come out of your mouth say one thing and your facial expression says another, anyone listening to you may have a hard time connecting with the words that you say. The gestures that you make on stage help add character to the words that you say. If you are giving a presentation and you stood perfectly still without a single movement or facial expression, you would look absurd. The same thing would happen if you use wild gesticulations. There has to be a balance between both extremes to keep the audience engaged and to effectively communicate with your audience.

A public speaker is a performer of sorts. They are not expected to use theatrics in the delivery of their role but there are techniques employed by stage performers that would prove very useful for a public speaker. Master these techniques; you will dominate the stage and keep your audience in your thrall. Remember, consistency in practice can make a difference. But that is not the only thing that we picked up from this chapter.

Public Speaking

To become a good public speaker, you must work on developing and mastering certain qualities. You should connect with your crowd, craft your stories masterfully and learn to control the rise and fall of your voice pitch.

To win over your crowd, you need to keep your content fresh. Use words that your audience would understand and be ready to change things at a moment's notice to accommodate the atmosphere of the crowd.

To showcase your wittiness, you only need to be yourself. Find out the unique aspect of you that people connect with the most and use that to your advantage

Finally, communication is everything. Your clothes, your confidence and your platform mean nothing if you are unable to get the right message across. Learn the technicalities of speech and practice daily.

Your tasks:

1. Learn at least three new words every day. Your learning of these words should include the meaning, the correct use in sentences as well as the correct

pronunciation of the words. The richer your vocabulary, the more articulate you become.
2. Practice four to five jokes before your next speech. Choose jokes that are appropriate for the event where you will be speaking.
3. This one is more of a suggestion than a task; consider taking a class in elocution or speech training. There are several online options.
4. Watch and take notes of the techniques of other public speakers. This is not so that you copy the way they do things exactly. This is to inspire you to do things a little differently from the usual.
5. Do exercises on facial expressions. The more exaggerated, the better. Your audience should be your mirror. Start with anger, curiosity and then keep going. The more expressions you master, the better your stage performance becomes.

CHAPTER NINE
MANAGING YOUR STAGE

"I'm about as monolingual as you come, but nevertheless, I have a variety of different languages at my command, different styles, different ways of talking which do involve different parameter settings."
Noam Chomsky

Movement for the Stage Novice

You may not be inclined to agree that your presence has more to do with performance than anything else but this is just one of those facts you are going to have to accept. There is an existing relationship between you and your audience. The audience may play dormant as the observer, but there is an unspoken dialogue that ensues and mastering your movement on stage can help you take charge of that conversation and lead it in the direction that you want it to go. Earlier on, we talked about confidence and body language. These are essential attributes that will help you make better use of your stage. Knowing how to move on that stage in the next step to maneuvering the stage to your advantage. I will start you off on the basics. Over time, the rest of it will come naturally to you.

1. Be deliberate in your actions

Every movement you make on stage should appear deliberate. Pacing the floors of your stage aimlessly would give negative feedback on your competency; random movements with no visual purpose would highlight your nervousness. Obviously, shuffling your feet among other unnecessary hand or foot movements is out of the question. A trick I like to use is to imagine that I have an invisible small cage around me restricting my range of movement. So, where my arms would extend out in a very wide gesture, I am consciously made to narrow my movements. This makes it appear less random and more deliberate.

2. Let your movement portray your message

If the speech you are giving has a motivational tone to it, the way that you move on stage should reflect this. Now, what do I mean by this? A motivational message is meant to inspire the listener to take action, right? Well, your movement should convey a sense of urgency to your audience that demands action. There should also be a lot of positive reinforcements using hand gestures. Let me give you a tiny but significant gesture that has a lot of impact in terms of the use of space and communication. When you point your index finger, you automatically create a focal point. Point it downwards, and you convey time (now, present, this moment), point it forward and your message takes a tone of responsibility (you are assigning responsibility). Point that same finger upwards and it can be interpreted as denoting authority.

3. Know where everything is

This has a much more practical function. You need to know where everything is in order to enhance your performance. This means that you have to arrive at the venue on time...perhaps while the organizers are still setting up so that you know where the equipment you might be using is going to be located. You don't want to get on stage and start fumbling around with the projector or trying to figure out where to put down any of the props you might need during the course of your presentation.

Speaking and Being Heard

There are many fancy tools these days that are used to make public speaking a much more impactful experience for both the audience and the speaker. But no tool is more powerful than your voice. Learn to control it and half your battle is won already. During a regular conversation, your voice takes on a regular tone. This way, you can be heard by the peers with whom you are having a conversation with and you don't need to increase your voice and make any extra effort to enunciate your words. On stage, the game is a little different. Not only do you need to project your voice, but you also need to enunciate your words carefully. To make matters worse, there is a very strong possibility that fear might make your voice sound a little coarser and hoarser than it naturally is. This is why you would find some people suddenly battling a coughing fit when they get on stage in an attempt to clear their throats.

To prevent this, here are some things you can do:

1. Take things slower

Trying to rush your words can seem as though you are trying to talk past the hot potato in your mouth. Your words are not clear and your pitch tends to be a little higher. Take a deep breath, exhale and then pace yourself while speaking. This will keep you within audible range and give your listeners an impression that you are knowledgeable on the subject. Speak slow, be loud (but not high pitched) and speak clearly.

2. Eat something before your presentation

Given the tension you feel in the pit of your stomach before you go on stage, some people worry about eating. The general fear is that they might throw up on stage. Except in very extreme cases, there is a slim to none chance of that happening. And contrary to how you feel, a light meal can go a long way to improving your performance on stage. I try to eat a high protein meal at least two hours before I get on stage. Not only does it make me feel energetic, I feel more alert.

3. Avoid cold things

A nervous sweat brought on by a nasty case of stage fright might have you reaching for iced water, but this can only make your voice coarse and thus make your stage experience worse. Warm water, lemon drops, and honey are excellent if you are already battling a sore throat but used on the regular, you can expect that your voice would be crisp and clear which is perfect for public speaking.

Turn Up the Drama

I did say earlier on that being on stage as a public speaker is somewhat like being a stage performer. You may not be theatrical but there are theatrical techniques you can employ to enhance your performance and engage your audience. Even if you are going to be reading your speech directly off a piece of paper, you still need to be able to know when to look up at the people you are reading it to. We already talked about being too monotonous in the delivery of your speech. The dramatics I am referring to here doesn't mean that you suddenly have to include pantomimes in your routines. It is about improving your sense of timing. A dramatic pause can create tension in a room so thick that as they say, you can cut through it with a knife.

To turn up the drama, you just need to do the following:

1. Talk confidently

Public Speaking

Injecting confidence into your voice even though you don't feel that way can bring a massive dose of drama to your presentation so that even though you are talking about quantum physics to a group of high school students, they would want to listen. It can take a lot of practice but if you keep at it, it will eventually come to you effortlessly.

2. Keep it short and sweet

People have a very short attention span. Waiting until the last minute to reveal your card might not work. Stir the drama by doing a quick introduction and then launching straight into the subject matter. This keeps your audience interested in what you have to pitch and sustains them to the end. Prolong things for longer than five minutes into your presentation and your big reveal may not even matter.

3. Don't complicate things

If you find yourself trying to explain your point five minutes after you made it, you probably have not done a good job in explaining it. Being dramatic in public speaking has little to do with complication. If you are speaking to people about makeup, there is no need to use terms specific to people in the aviation industry. You just end up confusing them. Use relevant colloquial terms to connect with your audience, convey your message and command their attention. Because at the end of the day, that is what the drama is all about.

Using the Stage for One

In acting, an actor would have to consider the presence of other people on stage and do his or her best to ensure that everyone gets their day in the spotlight. For a public speaker, you only share the stage with the idea you are hoping to get across. Other than that, the stage is really about you. Whether it is a big platform or a small podium, do your best to own it. Before you get on stage, you will be given a time limit. Do everything you can to ensure that you stay within this time limit and try not to think of it as a limit. For me, I like to think of it as a slice of time given to me to digest however I want to. Since most of my public speaking has had to do with training, I focus on driving my point home in that timeframe. To do this, I like to give bullet point presentations. This makes it easier to assimilate. I almost never use up my entire time, as I am more interested in interacting with my message than having them react to my message. I feel that if they interact with my message better, my point is driven home faster.

Set your own agenda for the time slot allocated to you and work that to your advantage. And most importantly, remember to have fun with the entire process. There is no rule that says that you can't. And if everything is looking a little too tedious for you, the next chapter breaks down how technology can be used to make your life that much easier. But first, to recap the contents of this chapter, let us go over what we have learned so far:

- Your movement on stage sets the tone for the kind of communication success you will achieve with your audience.
- Eating an hour or two before your presentation can keep you energetic and help you sustain an even tone of voice throughout. Starving yourself has the opposite effect.
- You need to employ the use of theatrical techniques to sustain the interest of your audience.
- The stage is designed for you to use as you will. Decide on your objectives and plan

towards achieving them within the timeframe that you are given.

Your tasks:

1. Besides making a name for yourself as a prominent public speaker, what are your objectives? Specifically, what do you expect to happen to your audience every time you get on stage? This will help you plan effectively.
2. Record yourself speaking. Listen to it, assess your performance and point out areas for improvement.
3. Practice your regular speech and a compressed version of this speech. This frees you up to be flexible if your time is suddenly cut short. This way, you can still have an impactful session with your audience.
4. Think of three possible questions that your audience might ask that will throw you off your game. Draft fresh and inspiring responses and then practice those responses.
5. Draft a response to a question that you may not have an answer to. Let the response be as fresh and inspiring as possible and then rehearse this also.

CHAPTER TEN
THE TOOLS OF THE TRADE

Fools ignore complexities. Pragmatists suffer it.
Some can avoid it. Geniuses remove it."

Alan Perlis

Coach Your Speed with Teleprompters

Technology is designed to make our lives easier and it is no different when it comes to public speaking. You can spend hours on end trying to rehearse a speech to help improve your stage performance and appear more authentic than choreographed to your audience. But what happens when you are called on to make an impromptu speech with not enough time to practice? Do you give up and miss out on an opportunity or do you step up to the challenge? Without enough practice, you may not feel confident to take the challenge, and this is where technology comes in. A teleprompter helps you in situations like this. Instead of keeping your head buried in the written speech on your paper, you are able to look up and deliver your speech. The teleprompter is actually quite popular in the oval office and in newsrooms, but it can come in handy on stage too.

Besides helping you with speech prompts, it can also help you with the precision of your words. I should point out here that while prompters are handy, they are best used in situations where establishing a connection is not as important as ensuring that the right message is passed across to your listener base, which may include more than those currently present in the room with you. That said, practicing your speech with a teleprompter can help you with your voice modulation and correct enunciation of your words. However, to avoid any awkward situation, you have to ensure that:

a) You have a printed version of the script. As with all machines, teleprompters can be problematic. If it suddenly goes off on you, you want to ensure that you are not frozen up in the middle of your speech.

b) Use cues to help you make the speech seem less robotic. Your teleprompter shouldn't have to mean a boring speech from start to finish. Infuse some excitement into your time slot by cueing yourself on the prompter to tell a story, a joke or engage the crowd in an activity.

c) Set the pace for the teleprompter. Certain prompters can only display a few lines at a time. If you don't set the pace, when you speak too slowly you get left behind, and if you speak fast there will be too many awkward silences. Rehearse the script at least once to give you an idea of how you want the timing to be like. Always remember, you take the lead.

Speech Training Apps

There is no law against improving your speech. As my dad always says whenever he gets an opportunity to learn, "I may be really good at what I do but there is always room for improvement." Speech training helps you become more articulate as a speaker and goes a long way in helping you perfect your craft. Thankfully, you can get these trainings right on your mobile device. These apps have a collective goal of helping you improve your public speaking skills but they do this differently. You may have to sample a few to determine what would work best for you. For this reason, I am going to highlight three of those apps. Not because I think that they are the best but because of the uniqueness of how they go about helping you become better as a public speaker.

1. The Simulator

Apps that fall in this category are designed to get you acquainted with the idea of speaking in front of a crowd by simulating the effect of a crowd. You may find the experience limiting, as an app can only do so much, but it does help you get over that initial fear and help you focus on your speech. An app that falls in this category is the ***public speaking simulator*** designed for iOS.

2. The Coach

These apps listen to your speech and offer pointers for improvement. Grammatical errors are corrected, practical tips for improvement are offered and areas where you sound repetitive are highlighted. While the focus is more on the technicalities of the speech than the delivery itself, it is a first step in helping to improve on the quality of your speech. The ***Ummo*** app is a good example of an app that can be grouped under speech coaching apps.

3. The Voice Tutor

After nailing the speech, you want to make sure that you get the delivery right on the money. It helps with issues like learning to pace yourself properly in terms of word flow and speech rhythm. "Pro Metronome" is an excellent app for this purpose. And this is available for both Android and iOS devices.

Compliment Your Presentation with Visual Aids

Typically, public speakers have had to rely on their gift of gab to paint a picture so vivid that it becomes etched in the minds of the audience. With the technological advancements of this age, you can use actual images to buttress your point. Using PowerPoint as a visual aid is an excellent tool. However, because you are going to have to divide the attention of your audience between yourself and the crowd, it becomes imperative that you take the lead and take the attention of the crowd where you want it to be at any point in time. Try these few tips to make a seamless transition:

1. Do not include your written speech in your presentation. This would only end up making the board the total focus at the speaking event. Instead, put bullet points with amazing facts on

the board and then expatiate on them as you scroll through each slide.

2. Use more imagery and fewer words. I believe that this is pretty self-explanatory. The idea is to get your audience to have fun with the session no matter how serious. At the very least, you want them to be engaged. Images do a good job of complementing what you are saying.

3. Keep the board interesting. Just because I said stick to using more images and fewer words doesn't mean you should go and complicate things with graphs, charts and mind-boggling figures. Save those for information that you can share with your audience after the presentation.

Timers to Keep You on Track

Timing is key in succeeding at public speaking and it is important that you utilize the time that you are given for maximum impact. Practicing your speech with a consciousness of time would ensure that you are able to effectively break down the information within that timeframe and as you master this, your confidence in your ability is being nurtured in the process. There are special devices designed for public speaking, but you can simply use your phone or even your wristwatch to get the ball rolling. Phones can sometimes interfere with the audio system so they may not be a good idea when you are on stage. But for practice, the stopwatch and timer features come in very handy. Some event organizers will install a timer that is visible from where you stand but not to the audience. Pay attention to it. This timer displays different colors to indicate when you are approaching your time limit and cue you in on when to wrap up. I do not advise that you wait until the last minute to wrap up. Give yourself at least five minutes to spare so that you don't feel hurried when you leave the stage. It speaks volumes about your competency, especially if this is a very formal setting.

In conclusion, technology can be your best friend. But you have to understand the basics in order to key into the benefits that a lot of these technology platforms would offer you. For starters:

Be clear about what you want to achieve and then look for technology that can support your goals. It would not make sense to go for the tech first because it mentions a few things related to what you want to do in the description. It is like going to buy a red shoe from the store in the hopes that it would become black. Before you subscribe, be sure that you are clear on how it would help you achieve your goals

Nothing can take the place of practice. No matter how efficient technology is, its level of efficiency is determined by how prepared you are.

Understand that even under the best circumstances, the unexpected happens. All of the careful planning and preparation you are putting into your next public speaking event is admirable but don't go in thinking that everything is going to go according to plan. Hope that it does but if it doesn't, this is one of those times that you are going to have to roll with the punches and learn from the experience.

CLOSING

"All is well that ends well."
William Shakespeare

There are no short cuts to attaining greatness and I believe that this book clearly illustrates this. The roads that you have taken so far and the places that you will have to navigate emotionally to get to the place that you desire will take you farther and farther away from who you used to be, and that is a good thing. You started this journey in your comfort zone and I am certain that in that time, you have undertaken at least one task that challenged your comfort. Public speaking can be easy or difficult. This depends on what angle you are looking at it from. This book was not written to resolve that debate. Rather, it is meant to give you a head start in running towards your goals.

The tasks written here are not one-off things that you can simply do and cross them off your to-do list. This is something that you are going to have to wake up and do every day, and decide to follow through on your promise to yourself to be better. I can talk this way because I have been exactly where you are. Desiring something so badly yet too afraid to seize it even when it is being presented to me on a platter of gold. Obviously, we know that you are not getting this on a platter of gold. You are going to have to work hard to earn every progressive step you make on this journey. There will be blood, sweat and frustration but that is what will make this all the more fulfilling when you make your way to the finish line, which would be on that stage as you exit to the sound of roaring applause. Of course, I am aware that you are not doing this for the cheering of the crowd, but it would not hurt if people acknowledged the greatness in you.

And even if the crowd has yet to recognize the greatness in you, I want you to recognize it because I am aware of it. Seeing as I have never met you before, how did I come to the conclusion that you are a great individual? For starters, the mere fact that you can dare to dream is an excellent indication. Secondly, seeing as you purchased this book as a next step to achieving your dreams tells me you have made up your mind to pursue your dream. If that doesn't speak to your greatness, I don't know what will. Your unique struggles with emotional issues like anxiety and absence of confidence in social settings even makes your ability to dream of

Public Speaking

becoming a public speaker that much more daring and interesting. They say that the only limitations we ever experience are in the mind. You have made the choice to break free from anything that will hold you back—and I salute that courage.

Silence the voices that question your fears and keep pushing until you break through. Thankfully, this is a field that celebrates your individuality. You just have to work up the courage to put yourself out there and own the space that you are given. If you need extra motivation, just bear in mind that the world is in dire need of innovative ideas and lending your voice to that process can bring us closer to developing the solution that might change the lives of people forever. I thank you for your time and consistency. And now, I look forward to seeing the many great and wonderful things you will do. Stay fresh, stay vibrant and most importantly, stay winning.

Thank you

Before you go, I just wanted to say thank you for purchasing my book.

You could have picked from dozens of other books on the same topic, but you chose this one.

So, a HUGE thanks to you for getting this book and for reading all the way to the end.

Now, I want to ask you for a small favor. **Could you please consider posting a review? Reviews are one of the easiest ways to support the work of independent authors.**

This feedback will help me continue to write the type of books that will help you get the results you want. If you enjoyed it, please let me know!

Lastly, don't forget to grab a copy of your free bonus book *"Bulletproof Confidence Checklist."* If you want to learn how to overcome shyness and social anxiety and become more confident, this book is for you.

Made in the USA
Middletown, DE
10 July 2023